The SOUND of My DAuGHtER'S VOiCE

The SOUND of My DAuGHtER'S VOiCE

WAYNE HASTINGS

Faith™ Parenting

Cook Communications

Faith Parenting is an imprint of
Cook Communications Ministries, Colorado Springs, Colorado
80918
Cook Communications, Paris, Ontario
Kingsway Communications, Eastbourne, England

Cover and Interior Design: iDesignEtc.
Cover Photo: The Stock Market
Editor: Gary Wilde

CIP data applied for

Contents

Dedication

This book is dedicated to Jennifer.
There can be something very special between
a father and his daughter, and I am so grateful to God that,
through Him, we are able to share
a deep, loving relationship.
You will always be the apple of my eye.

Acknowledgments

There are so many people to thank when you write such a deeply personal book. I want to begin by thanking Jesus Christ for all He has done to shape me into the parent He wants me to be. He is always there, to help and forgive, to teach and provide rest. Thank you.

My wife Pam is such an encourager and my soul mate. Thank you, Pam, for taking the time to help me, not only with this book, but with becoming a better parent. Your ability to help me clearly see where I could change my life for the better of our family, and your ability to love without reservation, are so remarkable. Thank you.

Pastors Bill Moore and Ron Salsbury are two men of God who understand the value of teaching people God's Word and His life-changing truth. Both of you helped me to think clearly and added insightful lessons. Thank you.

To my friends at Cook Communications, Randy Scott, Lee Hough, and Greg Clouse: I so appreciate your faith in this project and your constant encouragement. Thank you.

My prayer warrior friends are without a doubt where much of my strength came for this book. Joe, Suzanne, Del, Ginger, Steve, Bruce, and Dan: Thank you! God has certainly blessed me with a group of wonderful friends.

INTRODUCTION:

When a Voice Makes All the Difference

Christmas of 1998 was very different for us. For the first time in twenty-four years, my wife Pam and I spent an Advent season alone. Our son Zachary was in college and wouldn't arrive until the weekend before Christmas. Our daughter Jennifer and her new husband Deron lived in Madison, Wisconsin, and weren't due to arrive until the next day. The Christmas season was very different.

In years past, we spent many joyous times from Thanksgiving to New Year's. Pam is the tradition-maker in our family and, since the beginning of our marriage, she has made certain each holiday was full of uncommon delights and surprises. Christmas is her masterpiece as the whole house is specially lit, decorated, and made merry. She takes great pains to deliver such a holiday extravaganza. Her love of traditions helps us to immerse ourselves in the Advent season.

One of Pam's traditions was to include the whole family in the decorating. In years past, Dad and Zach took care of the tree, while Pam and Jennifer took care of the ornaments; men handled the outside illumination, and Pam and Jennifer dug out old decorations; Dad led evening Advent-focused Bible lessons, and away we went for maximum celebration of Jesus' birth. We even had a special time as each year we presented each of our children with an ornament. (Heaven help us if they decide they want them for their own trees; we'll need to purchase all new ornaments.)

Christmas of 1998, however, did not feature any of those unique traditions. Pam and I had to set up and decorate the tree. I had complete dominion over the lights. Pam took over the inside decorations, but her mood was not light, nor was mine. Our children were in other states, (we had just moved back to California from Michigan) and the burden of "Christmas setup" was our total responsibility. "Bah, Humbug!" was the cry, and we shed quite a few tears as well.

After all was said and done, all the tears shed, the memories remembered, we did it, but not with our usual happy hearts. We missed our kids, pure and simple. We missed the old traditions. We missed the laughter, the music playing, the new ornament opening, and we missed our family Bible studies during Advent.

When school break started, our kids arrived, (American Airlines has probably never experienced *that* much prayer in one day!) and the house immediately seemed to come alive. The decorations miraculously perked up, and the warm glow seemed to welcome our children back home. Warmth, prayer, celebration, food, and traditions all blended . . . and now, at last, we were ready to celebrate Christmas.

With the dawning of Christmas morning, Pam and I were, as usual, in the kitchen very early. Traditionally, Pam cooks a fine turkey, and it is my job to clean the bird before it's loaded with savory, herb-packed dressing and placed in the hot oven. As I was doing my best to clean Tom Turkey, I heard the wonderful voice (and a minute later the infectious laugh) of our daughter Jennifer. It seemed to echo throughout the house. The melodious, indescribable trill of this wonderful grown woman who means so much to me was bouncing off the walls once again. It was pure heaven on earth. Her voice added to our revived holiday spirit, and it got me to thinking and, of course, remembering.

What a Wonderful Voice!

Jennifer's voice reduced me to tears. I looked at Pam, and at that moment twenty-four years of Christmas celebrations, birthdays, and trips to Disneyland, vacations, and spontaneous ice cream excursions ran through the backwaters of my mind. Jennifer's laugh and the sound of her voice opened the floodgates of wonderful memories, and it deeply touched my heart. Instantly, I wanted to go back. I wanted to recreate all we had done and experienced in the past years. The sound of her voice took me to piano recitals, school plays, church plays, and math tutoring. Literally, everything that was Jennifer flashed by my tear-stained face. I was her dad, I had missed her, and I wanted desperately to return to "the golden days of yesteryear."

As I regained my composure, wiped some sympathetic tears from Pam's face, and began putting the finishing touches on the Christmas turkey, God spoke to me. It does not happen all that often, and maybe Jennifer's voice had softened me up enough to listen. Whatever happened, I listened to God and realized that our lives as parents had been wonderful. In fact, we are still parents, just in a different stage of life. Sure, the kids were not with us every day anymore, but we are still parents, and we still had a role to play in their lives. A different role, but a role nonetheless.

As I looked back, I realized that we experienced an incredible time rearing our children. Remember the movie *It's a Wonderful Life*? I don't claim to be George Bailey. George had some enviable characteristics, but they are not the point I want to make here. I do agree with the director, Frank Capra, though. Mr. Capra believed "that every man's life is important because it touches so many other lives."[1] Taking that a step further: *every parent's life is important because it touches so many children's lives.* We had a wonderful time rearing our children, and it became clear to me that I was being called to help other parents understand how we did it. To be able to share, from the heart, how two people, with little or no training, could rear such great kids is important today. Parents need some instruction and some practical handles so they can "touch" their children in a way that will encourage the kids and "train them up."

In Proverbs 22:6, God is saying two things. First, training

involves action and getting involved, and we parents can do it. Second, God gives us a picture of parents who *have a plan* to train and work with their children. Each stage may be a little different, each age may take different skills, and that's okay. What matters is that parents understand the needs of their kids and continually adjust their style of parenting to meet those needs. What an encouragement from God—get involved, you can do it, and have a plan for each stage.

The purpose of this book is to show parents these "stages" of a child's life. It is my hope that as you read this book that you'll determine where your kids are in life and learn to advance from one stage to another as they grow and change. In the spirit of Ecclesiastes 3, I have taken my life with Jennifer (and I throw in some about Zachary, as well) and spoken of them as special "times" in our lives as parents. Each "time" is associated with a span—a developmental period—in Jennifer's life. I have attempted to lay these times out chronologically. You may find, because of your particular circumstances with your children, that your "times" are different. Don't despair. I believe it is most important that you set your own course with your own children's internal clocks. I am suggesting that each of these "times" is important and will come into play at a certain stage in your child's life.

There is little doubt that parenting and fatherhood are a great challenge. I want this book to serve as a helping tool for you to see the importance and power of family values. I am not necessarily talking about the current politically correct term. I am talking about valuing your family. Every company has a value or a worth. The formula is simple: Assets minus liabilities equals net worth. Well, I believe a family has a value—a great value. The assets are the wonderful children God has blessed each of us with. The liabilities? To me, if we as parents don't reach out and get fully involved with our families, then we create the liabilities. The more we choose to get involved, the more we add to our family's value and worth.

The challenge to us is to become family leaders. We parents need to be the leaders of our homes and establish ourselves as mentors. We must be willing to positively influence our children's growth. James Dobson writes:

The current epidemic of self-doubt [in children] has resulted from a totally unjust and unnecessary system of evaluating human worth. This system is prevalent in our society. Not everyone is deemed worthy; not everyone is accepted. Instead, we reserve our praise and admiration for a select few who have been blessed from birth with characteristics we value most highly. It is a vicious system and we, as parents, must counterbalance its impact.[2]

Our involvement also helps to create traditions. Passing along a heritage of solid family values and leadership is an important legacy for our children. It is delightful to see Deron (our son-in-law) and Jennifer begin to create a home that has good traditions. We instilled in our children the value of traditions. God asked the Israelites to create memorial stones so they could remember His faithfulness. So too must we create traditions for our children to remember God's faithfulness and blessings to us.

It is my joy to share all of this with you. I love being a father, and it excites me to see my children mature. I want to share some ideas with you that should help you move your children to the next level. Eugene H. Peterson writes in *The Message,* "Point your kids in the right direction—when they're old they won't be lost" (Prov. 22:6).

It is my burning desire that this book gives you a tool to point your children in the right direction, and a tool to help you be an effective parent.

God bless you,

Wayne Hastings
February, 2000

Notes

1 Frank Capra, *It's a Wonderful Life*, words on video jacket.

2 James Dobson, *The New Hide and Seek* (Grand Rapids, MI: Fleming H. Revell, 1999), p. 23.

BIRTH–
A TIME FOR JOY

Chapter 1

ALL OF US NINTH-GRADERS had to do an extensive report on our futures. The project was called an Occupational Notebook, and we needed to project ourselves ten to fifteen years into the future, choosing a college, career, lifestyle, and a place of residence. What fun to read those reports aloud at the end of the year!

I had forgotten about the Notebook until we recently moved from Michigan to California. Unpacking one of the boxes, I found it, took a little break from the "fun" of unpacking, and read that report for the first time in quite awhile.

What surprised me was the lifestyle section. Here I was, a father of two wonderful children, yet as I read the Notebook, I had said nothing at all about children. According to my ninth-grade vision, I wasn't even married. I was single, driving a Jaguar XKE, and living in Phoenix!

Now, my wife, when she caught me taking a break, read the report and said, "Look at it this way, Wayne, most ninth-grade boys don't think about marriage." She may be right, but we'd been *assigned* to think about it, and as I talked with her, I realized that I just couldn't remember considering the idea of having children. It had simply been out of the question for me.

Now, being a father and looking back, I don't know what I'd do without my children. Over the years, they've given me unbelievable pleasure (and yes, some pain) and taught me so many lessons. Therefore, the moral of this story is this—*if I can do this parenting thing, then anybody can.* So please be encouraged that someone who never thought he would be a parent actually is a parent . . . and loves it!

Parenting is work, no doubt about that. However, the rewards far exceed the effort. But we can't approach it haphazardly. There are, I believe, certain steps that parents need to adopt in order to rear their children effectively. Let's look at those steps, starting at birth in this chapter and then moving to other "times" as this book unfolds.

New Baby, Long Drive Home

The first time I heard my daughter's voice, it was beautiful to me, even though it was the sound of crying. When Jennifer was born, the local hospital didn't allow fathers into the delivery room, so I didn't get to hear her very first cry. (To this day, I feel I was robbed of a wonderful experience.) I was able to be there when our son Zachary was born, but with Jennifer, I was the pacing father in the waiting room, begging the hours to pass more quickly in the middle of the night. I watched the hands on the clock as they refused to move until—finally!—a short, red-haired goddess with a white cap walked over to me flashing the most incredible smile: "It's a nice, healthy, chubby little girl, Mr. Hastings! Mother and Daughter are doing just fine." I could have jumped out of my skin with delight. I was a father!

Wait a minute. . . . I'm a father? *What in the world do I do now?*

Actually, at that moment, there wasn't a thing to do. I briefly saw Pam and went to my parents' house to announce the news and get some sleep. When I awoke, we were all happy, but I still had this nagging thought, *Me, a father?*

It really sunk in as we were driving Jennifer home from the hospital. That's when I heard her first cry. We were so nervous! I drove like a very senior citizen. Pam held on to that little bundle so tightly. And, of course, Jennifer just cried and cried, all the way home. Nothing we did seemed to help.

Arriving home didn't help.

Walking Jennifer up and down the hallway didn't help.

Talking to her like a clown didn't help.

Making cute faces like a baby camel didn't help.

Standing on my head juggling boiled eggs didn't help.

(What have you tried? Believe me . . . it doesn't help.)

Pam was so patient, but I was a nervous wreck!

Over the next few weeks we became more settled, and Jennifer became the center of our attention. I still didn't have a clue as to what I needed to do—what was this fatherhood stuff all about? Pam seemed to be a good mother, but what was I doing?

As time progressed, Pam increasingly became a great mother, but I was drifting. Then one evening Pam and I had a long talk. She was frustrated with my seeming lack of support of her and her new mothering role. She needed my help, and she told me that I also had a role to play in rearing our new baby.

Looking back, I can see that at that moment an important lesson emerged for me and for all parents: *Birth is a time for taking up responsibility, the responsibility of serving.* It is a time for a husband to serve his wife, and it is a time for a father to begin learning how to serve his child.

The Joy of Responsibility

Charles Kingsley once said, "Do today's duty . . . and don't weaken and distract yourself by looking forward to things that you can't see and couldn't understand if you saw them." [1] His words sum up what I was doing. Things I couldn't see were distracting me, and they were things I couldn't understand. Of course, I wasn't expected to be the perfect parent the moment we brought Jennifer home from the hospital. All Pam expected of me was to take responsibility—to serve her and Jennifer.

Look at how the wise men responded to Jesus' birth. Matthew 2:10 says, "And when they saw the star they rejoiced exceedingly with great joy" (KJV). Then they chose to take responsibility. They chose to respond to God's leading by doing something new, difficult, and a bit scary. When we're faced with new or difficult situations, we can choose to respond in a number of ways. The story of Jesus' birth suggests at least three options:

• *We can react with fear.* When new circumstances come along, we can pull back in fear. In my first book, *Trusting Enough to Parent,* I defined FEAR as Future Events Appearing Real. When we fail to TRUST (Truly Rely on Scriptural Truth) but instead look ahead at a circumstance or a challenge and let our imaginations control us to the point of inaction or escapism, then we're wallowing deep in the trenches of fear. King Herod, in the first few chapters of Matthew is a great biblical example of FEAR. Matthew 2:3 tells us he was "disturbed" by the news. In verse 7, he called the Magi together "secretly." In verse 16, he was "furious and he gave orders to kill all the boys in Bethlehem and its vicinity who were two years old and under" (NIV). Talk about fearful! This reprehensible ruler certainly wasn't taking up his God-given responsibility to serve. Remember: The best way to conquer FEAR is to TRUST.

• *We can turn away with indifference.* This is the second way we can respond when life's challenges crash in upon us and upset our routines. Throughout the Gospels, we see the religious leaders of Jesus' day acting apathetically to the message of a whole new kingdom that should have turned their world upside down. They didn't want that to happen, though! Here is God's Son among humankind, and all the religious leaders can do is question Him, turning away from the gift God had given them. "These priests knew the Scriptures and pointed others to the Savior, but they would not go to worship Him themselves! They quoted Micah 5:2 but didn't obey it. They were five miles from the very Son of God, yet they didn't go to see Him!" [2]

On vacation this year, I was saddened to see how many parents seemed indifferent toward their children. Pam and I went to a popular place for family vacations and, time after time, we saw fathers and mothers who were simply unresponsive to their children. Family members were all together as a group, but the level of indifference was so high that only a few repeated patterns of physical resemblance—maybe the cute pug noses, or the jumbo ears, or the curly black locks—made it seem that the kids and parents were related at all. But biological cloning is not family life! Remember: The best way to conquer INDIFFERENCE is to GET INVOLVED.

• *We can move into joy.* The wise men decided to be joyful with this new circumstance. These men were Gentiles, yet they joyfully chose to go and worship Jesus. The Magi were seeking the King; Herod was opposing the King; and the religious leaders were ignoring the King.

Oswald Chambers wrote once that happiness depends on what happens and joy does not. Joy is an inner peace and stillness that helps us focus on what we should do, while neither looking ahead or behind. It grows out of sincere worship of God. In worship the Lord encourages us to take a "time out" from everything else to focus on thankfulness, to celebrate and enjoy all He has given us, and to let our gratitude move us into servanthood. Remember: JOY leads to SERVING.

The other two responses, fear and indifference, lead us into escape and noninvolvement. Joy, on the other hand, leads us into God's presence and frees us to serve. When we respond as the Magi responded, we carve out for ourselves a wonderful experience of serving. The Magi recognized the gift God had given the world, and they gave back to God in wonder and worship. They chose to serve.

Like the wise men, parents need to examine their response to parenthood. The Magi responded to God's leading, experienced great joy, and decided to serve. Parents who respond out of indifference or FEAR don't have the opportunity of joy. Chances are the wise men left their encounter with Christ changed men and content with what they had done. Parents who face the new responsibility with joy feel the same contentment and also gain tremendous benefit from being with their children.

The Joy of Serving

Every stage of our children's lives is a time for parents to serve. It hit me hardest just after we brought Jennifer home from the hospital. I needed to get involved, and I needed to respond with joy and to learn how to serve both my wife and my new daughter. Second Timothy 2:24-26 (KJV) reads:

> *The servant of the Lord must not strive but be gentle unto all men, apt to teach, patient, in meekness instructing those that oppose themselves; if God peradventure will give them repentance to the acknowledging of the truth; And that they may recover themselves out of the snare of the devil, who are taken captive by him at his will.*

The verse is sound advice from Paul to his beloved Timothy. He is saying, "Be a servant and stop fighting. Be gentle and patient, and instruct people who don't have a clue as to what's right or wrong." In other words, take responsibility, stop fighting with people, find joy, and serve.

Paul tells Timothy that false teaching will always be divisive, but the Lord's servant should not be a fighter but a promoter of unity, by being kind ("gentle") to everyone. Such servants will be forbearing in the face of conflict or ill treatment. The Lord's servant must treat even his opponents with gentle instruction characterized by "meekness" (gentleness with humility).

Parents aren't normally fighting an enemy, of course. Sometimes, however, battling our rotten attitudes and fiery emotions can be just as tough as defending a battlefield fortress from a devastating mortar barrage. Yes, the shrapnel can fly in any family, and I'm sure you've taken more than a little flak already! But in cases where emotions are running white hot, we're called to set our own needs aside and to simply serve. Paul reminds Timothy that being gentle, humble, and "ready to bear evil-treatment without resentment" are hallmarks of someone committed to serving others.

I love sports and have played them all my life. At the time our daughter was born, I was playing golf almost weekly. I was also on a league softball team that had games at least weekly, if not twice a week. I was busy doing my own thing and, using Paul's words, fighting the change that had come into my life. I sure didn't want to give up my sports.

Pam and I talked about it (more than likely quarreled a few times about it), and over time I realized that I wasn't serving my family to the best of my ability. Therefore, I decided to put softball and golf on the shelf. Now, in retrospect, I wouldn't trade the family time I created by this decision for any string of holes-in-one or home runs. I can vividly remember some very special times with both Jennifer and Zachary that I probably would have lost if I'd been so self-absorbed in those hobbies that kept me away from home.

Saturday, around our house, became Dad's day. Almost every Saturday, I took over from Pam and spent time with the kids. From the days he began walking, Zachary would join me in mowing the lawn. He walked right beside me, holding onto the mower (and living in Southern California meant lots of lawn mowing). Those memories will be with me forever. I learned to be a servant to my kids' needs, being there for them and enjoying every moment.

Putting Yourself . . . Last

Remember this old Sunday School song?

> *J.O.Y., J.O.Y. Tell you what it means:*
> *Jesus first, yourself last, and others in between.*

This cute little ditty is actually an eloquent symphony of

basic servant-living theology. It puts into simple (and hard to forget) words the action a servant must take if he is to truly serve others. Look closely at the example of Jesus. He came down from heaven and freed the world's people, not Himself. He did the will of the Father and put Himself last. Can anyone imagine the anguish He must have felt? Can anyone truly understand what it meant to be King of Kings and die like a common thief?

We can, however, learn the lessons of Christ. One in particular that needs to be front and center is the idea of putting ourselves last. Isaiah 42 describes the coming Messiah. The passage begins:

> *¹ Here is my servant, whom I uphold, my chosen one in whom I delight; I will put my Spirit on him and he will bring justice to the nations.*
> *² He will not shout or cry out, or raise his voice in the streets.*
> *³ A bruised reed he will not break, and a smoldering wick he will not snuff out. In faithfulness he will bring forth justice;*
> *⁴ he will not falter or be discouraged till he establishes justice on earth. In his law the islands will put their hope.*
>
> —Isaiah 42:1-4 (NIV)

Not only is God describing the Messiah, but He is also describing the qualities of a servant. Consider them with me:

• *God delights in His servant.* It is for His pleasure that we serve. When we put God's plan to work and serve others (our children and families in this case) we are not looking for personal glory or esteem. As we seek to please Him, God delights in our sacrifice and dedication.

• *God energizes His servant.* God puts His Spirit on him, and in so doing, provides the energy for every task. Having a servant's heart is never easy, yet God in His wisdom energizes the servant to carry out His will. God energizes us for servant-like action.

- *God quiets His servant.* A true servant of the Lord doesn't need to shout his or her accomplishments from the housetops. True servants do their work quietly and with one purpose in mind—to glorify God and work out His will. When we dedicate our lives to serving others, God calms our heart and shows us that in quietness we are shouting His praise.

- *God empowers His servant.* How easy it would be for us to attempt all of this our own strength! God, however, gives us the willingness to be gentle and dependent while accomplishing His purposes. How tempting it would be to do the obvious—but no, God empowers us to maintain focus and look to Him for each succeeding step.

- *God balances His servant.* God provides His faithful servant with a unique support system. God provides wisdom to judge situations and acts as the fulcrum between fatigue and despair. The servant sees so much to do all around him; he needs God's full support. God helps the servant maintain equilibrium at all times.

The culmination of God's work in the servant's heart is hope and justice. Perhaps not the justice we see on *Court TV*, but a justice driven by God's law and by the attitude of the servant's heart. Furthermore, the hope lies not in what we can do alone, but what we can do as a servant controlled by a loving God who provides exactly what we need to be the servant-leader of our homes. Bible commentator William Barclay said:

> *There are always two ways of doing things. A man can do the irreducible minimum and not a stroke more; he can do it in such a way as to make it clear that he hates the whole thing; he can do it with the barest minimum of efficiency and no more; or he can do it with a smile, with a gracious courtesy, with a determination, not only to do this thing, but to do it well and graciously. He can do it, not simply as well as he has to, but far better than anyone has any right to expect him to. The inefficient workman, the resentful servant, the ungracious helper have not even begun to have the right idea of the*

Christian life. The Christian is not concerned to do as he likes; he is concerned only to help, even when the demand for help is discourteous, unreasonable and tyrannical.[3]

Putting Others First

If the servant attitude demands that we put ourselves last, it is only natural, then, to put others first. Yet it's one of those things easier said than done.

The Robin Williams movie *Hook* provides a good example of what can happen. Robin plays Peter Banning, a successful attorney and businessman. He can't seem to separate himself from his office or his clients. He has a son who plays baseball and wants his father to see him play. Peter, however, puts everything else first and doesn't get to see his son play ball.

As the story unfolds, we discover that Peter Banning is actually the grown-up Peter Pan. He and the family go to visit Granny Wendy Darling and the legendary Captain Hook kidnaps Peter's son. Peter Banning returns to never-never land only to discover that Captain Hook has stolen his son's affections. Why? Because Hook was smart enough to realize that if he paid attention to the boy—seemingly giving him love—that he could turn him against his father.

The movie ends with a marvelous scene in which Peter Pan-Banning learns the true value of putting his son first. He quickly disposes of the motley Captain Hook and returns home a changed man with his priorities straight. Peter Pan-Banning learns the power of putting others' needs first. The Gospel of Mark reads:

> [33] *After they arrived at Capernaum, Jesus and his disciples settled in the house where they would be staying. Jesus asked them, "What were you discussing out on the road?"*
> [34] *But they didn't answer, because they had been argu-*

ing about which of them was the greatest.
³⁵ He sat down and called the twelve disciples over to him. Then he said, "Anyone who wants to be the first must take last place and be the servant of everyone else."
—Mark 9:33-35 (NLT)

This Scripture, above any others, reveals how the disciples didn't yet realize who Jesus was and what He expected from them. Repeatedly He had told them what awaited Him in Jerusalem, and yet they were still thinking of His Kingdom in earthly terms and of themselves as His heads of state. How many times do we miss the point? We spend our time thinking about the absolute wrong thing while our child is saying, "Hey, I'm hurting! Pay attention to my needs, not whether or not you are going to make it!"

The disciples, like many parents, knew they were wrong. When Jesus asked them what they had been arguing about, they had nothing to say. It was the silence of shame. They had no defense. Just like Peter Pan-Banning, parents know what they should do, yet they're caught up in something else that seems more important for the moment. According to William Barclay:

Jesus dealt with this very seriously. It says that he sat down and called the Twelve to Him. When a Rabbi was teaching as a Rabbi, as a master teaches his scholars and disciples, when he was really making a pronouncement, he sat to teach. Jesus deliberately took up the position of a Rabbi teaching His pupils before He spoke. And then He told them that if they sought for greatness in His Kingdom they must find it, not by being first but by being last, not by being masters but by being servants of all. It wasn't that Jesus abolished ambition. Rather He recreated and sublimated ambition. For the ambition to rule He substituted the ambition to serve. For the ambition to have things done for us He substituted the ambition to do things for others.⁴

Doesn't this make sense? What truly great men do you know who put themselves first? Rather they find ways of helping others be successful. While living in our first home, we had wonderful neighbors. Bill Ashcraft was a fine man who willingly gave, from his heart, everything he had. Pam and I were newly married, low on money, and very naïve. Bill, however, was always ready to help us. Whether it was lending me tools or teaching me how to fix things around the house, Bill was always there for my family and me. He knew what it meant to be a servant and put others first.

British Prime Minister Stanley Baldwin paid a noble tribute to Lord Curzon when Curzon died. He said:

> *I want, before I sit down, to say one or two things that no one but I can say. A Prime Minister sees human nature bared to the bone, and it was my chance to see him twice when he suffered great disappointment—the time when I was preferred to him as Prime Minister, and the time when I had to tell him that he could render greater service to the country as chairman of the Committee of Imperial Defence [sic] than in the Foreign Office. Each of these occasions was a profound and bitter disappointment to him, but never for one moment did he show by word, look, or innuendo, or by any reference to the subject afterwards, that he was dissatisfied. He bore no grudge, and he pursued no other course than the one I expected of him, of doing his duty where it was decided he could best render service.[5]*

Here was a man whose greatness lay not in the fact that he reached the highest offices of state, but in the fact that he was ready to serve his country anywhere.

True selflessness is rare, but it is remembered when it is found. The ancient Greeks told the story of a Spartan named Paedaretos. Three hundred men were to be chosen to govern Sparta, and Paedaretos was a candidate. However, in the end, his name wasn't on the list. "I am sorry," said one of his friends, "that you were not elected. The people ought to have known what a wise officer of state you would have made."

"I am glad," said Paedaretos, "that in Sparta there are three hundred men better than I am." Here was a man who became a legend because he was prepared to give to others the first place and to bear no ill will.

How many problems could be solved if men and women lived for what they could do for others and not only for what they could get for themselves? Jesus gives not only the disciples a great lesson but us parents as well. We must strive to be last—by putting our children first.

The Joy of Thanksgiving

What a Gift!

And the LORD God formed a man's body from the dust of the ground and breathed into it the breath of life. And the man became a living person.
—Genesis 2:7 (NLT)

Not only do parents need to respond to and serve their children, early in their childrens' lives parents should develop a sense of deep thankfulness for the absolute miracle of birth. Just contemplate that miracle for a moment. Two people, in love, create another human being. The result of that unbelievable process is a gift from God.

When Jennifer was born, we took her to church as soon as possible. Like most babies, she cried, and most of the time she cried when we didn't want her to. Church was no exception. In an effort to quiet her and also help my wife, I'd take Jennifer in my arms and hold her in front of me. I'd place her head in one hand and her bottom in the other. Then, like a weightlifter doing arm curls, I'd gently rock my little girl—up and down. In those private, tender moments, I realized every Sunday what a special gift I was holding. She would look up into my eyes and we connected. With some prayer from Daddy, she would drift to sleep and I'd continue to hold this precious gift from God. Today, even though Jennifer has grown up and has a husband, I still look into those brown eyes and see God's gift. *The Life Application Bible Notes* remind us:

> *"From the dust of the ground" implies that there is nothing fancy about the chemical elements making up our bodies. The body is a lifeless shell until God brings it alive with his "breath of life." When God removes his life-giving breath, our bodies once again return to dust. Therefore, our life and worth come from God's Spirit. Many boast of their achievements and abilities as though they were the originator of their own strengths. Others feel worthless because their abilities don't stand out. In reality, our worth comes not from our achievements but from the God of the universe, who chooses to give us the mysterious and miraculous gift of life. Value life, as he does.* [6]

How Special and Unique!

> *O LORD, what a variety of things you have made! In wisdom you have made them all. The earth is full of your creatures.*
>
> —Psalm 104:24 (NLT)

Not only should we be thankful for the special gifts God has given us in our children, we must also recognize that they are special and unique individuals. Too many parents make the mistake of trying to forge their children's identity out of their own, and God simply does not have that purpose in mind with creation. The psalmist reminds us that God has created a variety of things, not simply clones. God created unique and special children to do His will and increase His kingdom.

In a later chapter we will take a more detailed look at the uniquenesses of our children. For now, it's important just to learn to be thankful for each child's special and unique qualities.

I remember looking at Jennifer for the first time. Whom did she look like? What color would her eyes be? For us, her hair was the main attraction. Now, I must say that Jennifer was a bald baby, and it took awhile for her to actually grow some hair. However, when she did begin to grow hair, it was a beautiful auburn-red color. Neither Pam nor I have red hair, so this certainly made Jennifer unique and special.

One day, when Jennifer was just a little girl, someone asked her where she got her red hair. Jennifer, who was never unwilling to talk, said, "From the mailman." Now, let me set the record straight, the mailman had nothing to do with it! However, that is how striking a contrast it was for us to have a redhead in the family.

Not only are our children special and unique physically, God has given each a temperament that may be different from our own. Our children certainly don't bear the identical personality or temperament characteristics that we do. Jennifer is much like me, but much more outgoing. Zachary has a temperament much like his mother's, but he is more detail-oriented.

The point is, we just couldn't put our children in a box, especially a box we wanted to create for them. God makes them unique, and we need, early on, to fully appreciate that and praise God for His wisdom.

A Great Blessing!

> "Don't be frightened, Mary," the angel told her, "for God has decided to bless you!"
>
> —Luke 1:30 (NLT)

Yes, the birth of Jesus would cause pain. He would eventually leave His mother and be killed by a crowd of people for crimes He didn't commit. That had to be very difficult on Mary, and although she didn't know that at this time, she is told even before conception that God had decided to bless her. She is to be the Savior's mother.

God, however, blesses all parents, not just Mary. Those precious little gift-bundles may cause some pain, but the rewards of guiding our children into maturity far exceed the pain. Now consider with me three specific, biblical reasons why children are such a blessing:

1. *They are God's own.* Romans 8:16-17 reads, "The Spirit Himself bears witness with our spirit that we are children of God, and if children, heirs also, heirs of God and fellow heirs with Christ, if indeed we suffer with Him in order that we may also be glorified with Him" (NASB). God seeks our children and makes them his own. They are special to Him.

2. *They are God's heritage.* Psalm 127:3-5 reads, "Behold, children are a gift of the LORD; the fruit of the womb is a reward. Like arrows in the hand of a warrior, so are the children of one's youth. How blessed is the man whose quiver is full of them; They shall not be ashamed, when they speak with their enemies in the gate" (NASB). To a Jewish family, marriage was a "bank" into which God dropped precious children who were His investment for the future; it was up to the father and mother to raise those children in the fear of God. Children were rewards, not punishments; opportunities, not obstacles. They aren't burdens; they are investments that produce dividends.

3. *They are God's examples.* Mark 10:13-16 reads, "And they were bringing children to Him so that He might touch them; and the disciples rebuked them. However, when Jesus saw this, He was indignant and said to them, 'Permit the children to come to Me; don't hinder them; for the kingdom of God belongs to such as these. Truly I say to you, whoever does not receive the kingdom of God like a child shall not enter it at all.' And He took them in His arms and began blessing them, laying His hands upon them" (NASB).

Children are wonderful examples of trust and dependence. They come to Jesus with pure hearts and with wide-eyed excitement of faith. They can be such blessings to parents as they approach life with the same qualities. God uses children as an example of how all of us should approach Him—trusting, depending, pure, and excited.

The joy of thanksgiving then is a unique thankfulness for the gift with which God has so richly blessed us. It is an appreciation and thankful heart for the unique and special children He has given us, and a realization of the blessing that children bring.

Let Yourself Enjoy It!

Birth brings with it a new set of responsibilities as well as joys. There is nothing more important for parents to do than to understand the joy of God's gift and the importance of rearing their children in a way that is fully dependent upon the Lord and the principles of His Word. Experiencing the joy of parenting will clearly exceed anything you have ever done in your life. Just consider—

Builders. Do you like building things? Do you like creating a design, deciding on the raw materials necessary, and then creating the plans that detail the specifications? Do you like to put it together? Do you enjoy standing back and seeing the final product?

If you answered "yes" to any or all of these questions, parenting will be your greatest building project. With children, you can spend a lifetime creating, building, and looking at the results. You can plan, you can finely sand, you can stroke the smooth edges and see your creation develop right in front of your eyes. Rearing children will be your ultimate building project.

Gardeners. Do you like growing things? Do you like planting seeds? Do you enjoy cultivating, weeding, and watering? Do you enjoy watching seedlings turn into plants? Do you take pleasure in smelling the roses once they bloom?

If you answered "yes" to any or all of these questions, parenting will be your best garden. With children, you're planting the seeds of potential adulthood. You'll water them and watch them grow into trees of strong character. You can gently prune the branches and discipline them to produce wonderfully sweet-smelling flowers and breathtaking fruit. Rearing children will be your finest garden.

Quilters. Do you enjoy finding just the right fabric to make attractive squares? Do you look for unique designs and then begin to patch in the squares? Do you seek the warmth of a new quilt, so soft to the touch?

Rearing children will be your best-ever quilt. With children, you can find the uniquenesses and reward them. You can encourage children and help them patch together their lives to develop a design that is uniquely theirs. Children give lots of love, and their warmth is immeasurable. Children will be your most luxurious quilt.

Leaders. Do you enjoy bringing people together to form a solid team? Do you like helping people reach their potential? Do you set goals? Do you enjoy mentoring?

Rearing children will be the best leadership project you have ever undertaken. With your children, you can assemble the best team ever. You can use effective team leadership skills and help children develop their strengths within the team. You can mentor every day and see life-changing results. You can work with your children to set goals and celebrate with them as they achieve them.

Everyone. At birth, your child's voice may be the sound of a piercing cry or it may be a soft cooing. Whatever the sound, take time to be grateful for the joy that has just entered your life. Take time to savor the joy of responding to the new life that has entered your home. Take time to appreciate the joy of serving that new life. Take time to delight in the joy of thanking God for such a gift, such a blessing, and such a unique individual.

Children are an inheritance from the Lord. Be joyful!

Notes

1 Charles Kingsley, in *Draper's Book of Quotations for the Christian World*, 1992, #9650.

2 Warren Wiersbe, "Be" Series, NT, Volumes 1 & 2 (Colorado Springs: Cook Communications, 1989).

3 William Barclay, *Daily Study Bible—New Testament* (Louisville: Westminster John Knox Press, 1975).

4 Ibid.

5 Ibid.

6 Notes and Bible helps from *New Testament Life Application Notes and Bible Helps* (Wheaton, IL: Tyndale House). *Harmony of the Gospels* copyright 1986 by James C. Galvin.

TODDLER–
A TIME TO JOIN

℞
Chapter 2

AS JENNIFER MOVED FROM INFANCY to toddlerhood, the sound of her voice became a babbling of excitement. What adventures she had exploring everything! She learned to do an enormous number of things in a very short space of time. Infants or toddlers will start to walk with feet a little apart to remain steady at first, to run—beginning awkwardly—to kneel, and to climb on stairs. As they develop better muscle control, they enjoy more climbing and can manage a low slide and swing. They can push, pull, and jump, and may be starting to throw and kick balls.

At this age, the adventure continues as many toddlers can build towers of play bricks and learn balancing. Their hands become more skilled at holding and moving things, and they may be able to use plastic scissors, under supervision, to practice cutting. (Don't expect them to be good at this; just let them enjoy snipping out rough shapes.)

Most toddlers really begin to enjoy music, and they can take pleasure in moving to the sounds of melodies and rhythms. Many times Jennifer and I'd "dance" around our house to loud, beat-driven music. I'd hold her in my arms and she would throw herself backwards and forwards in my arms. She could also bang out beats using pots, pans, or anything else that made a loud sound.

At this point, toddlers can begin dressing themselves. But

like everything else I have said about this age, they will need supervision and help. Toddlers also need lots and lots of encouragement as they try out new things and make mistakes. Learning to walk is just a series of falls, with more and more space in between them. Dressing or building is simply one "failure" after another. So encouragement serves a great purpose—it boosts their confidence and ability to try, try again.

I say all this because toddlers demand a lot of energy from their parents. It's a time of great learning and exploration for the toddler. Parents need six hands and four legs to keep up with this exploring, excessively curious mass of energy.

Parents, having toddlers in your home means lots of teamwork! It's a time when we need to make a decision to fully join the ranks of committed parenting. I made the mistake of not joining the ranks, and I paid dearly for it. For some reason, I again let Pam take care of Jennifer's every need during those years. When I'd get home from work, Pam would be exhausted. Yet Jennifer, after awhile, wanted only her mother. One night, Pam confronted me with the problem: once again, I just wasn't part of the team. I hadn't made a commitment to join the ranks.

Please Join the Ranks!

Recruiting posters, especially during the Second World War, have made some interesting marketing pleas. "Join the Navy, and see the world," one promised. Or recall the infamous, "Uncle Sam wants YOU"—with the picture of our dear old "uncle," finger pointing straight at us. The country needed soldiers and sailors, and the posters told the story quickly and efficiently, with a theme of "let's get going because we have a job to do." Today, the Internet literally screams messages at us to "join." Whether it's making a certain portal your home page, or signing up for a "free" e-mail newsletter, the Internet, at times, seems like a continuous billboard calling users to join, join, join.

Like one of those posters, or a favorite Internet site, Pam strongly encouraged me to join the team. There was a battle going on—Jennifer's energy level and ability to move around was increasing and I wasn't there to help or to see the changes in Jennifer. Pam told me she was tired and that it was time I took some of the responsibility. I may not have seen the trouble, but once Pam confronted me and shared her heart with me, it was easy to understand that I was making a huge mistake. I made a decision (which really became a lifelong one) to get going and join the family team. She'd put out a call for me to join; I enlisted for the full term.

Jesus Recruited a Great Team

Jesus, as He does so frequently, gives us a good model for joining the ranks:

> [18] *And walking by the Sea of Galilee, He saw two brothers, Simon who was called Peter, and Andrew his brother, casting a net into the sea; for they were fishermen.*
> [19] *And He said to them, "Follow Me, and I will make you fishers of men."*
> [20] *And they immediately left the nets, and followed Him.*
> [21] *And going on from there He saw two other brothers, James the son of Zebedee, and John his brother, in the boat with Zebedee their father, mending their nets; and He called them.*
> [22] *And they immediately left the boat and their father, and followed Him.*
>
> —Matthew 4:18-22 (NASB)

• *He called them from the familiar.* Jesus approached these men and asked them to leave what they knew and to join Him in something they knew nothing about. He made no promises or guarantees of success, riches, or social status. These men were fishermen, not evangelists. They hadn't been studying rabbinical law for years, or public relations, or oration. They were fishermen.

Jesus called them from the familiar and had to equip them

for their new mission. Within just three years He needed to instill what He believed and what He expected of these men. Remember that, in those days, the training of persons for spiritual leadership in Judaism required that learners serve as apprentices, or disciples, of recognized teachers.

A rabbi's disciple literally lived with his teacher, accompanying him everywhere. He learned not only by listening to his master's teaching but also by observing his actions. . . . Becoming a particular teacher's disciple was a life-shaping decision. In addition, it was just as important to the teacher to carefully select his disciples. For while the disciple expected the relationship with his master to shape as well as equip him, the master would be honored for the piety of his students, and he would have to depend on them to pass on any distinctive teachings of his own to future generations.[1]

Jesus called His disciples from the familiar in order to do something they hadn't been prepared to do. He called them from the familiar into a life of change. Parents are often called from the familiar as well. I was an only child and never had the opportunity to be around infants or toddlers. I was ill-equipped for what was ahead.

• *He called them to change.* This isn't the first time we see in the Bible that God asks someone to change. Psalm 78:70-72 (NIV) reads:

He chose David his servant and took him from the sheep pens; from tending the sheep he brought him to be the shepherd of his people Jacob, of Israel his inheritance. And David shepherded them with integrity of heart; with skillful hands he led them.

God frequently asks us to change. He asked the disciples to leave the familiar and become "fishers of men." In the Old Testament, He asked David to leave his sheep and become a shepherd of the people of Israel. He called the soon-to-be-appointed disciples to a higher level of fishing, just as he called David to a higher level of shepherding. God asked them to change, but He also knew them well. He knew that they (both the disciples and David) had the tools necessary to change and to reach this higher level.

• *He gave them something new.* Jesus didn't just take away the old; He also gave something new. God is good at that. When He gives us something new, it usually encourages us, moves us, and motivates us. He takes old thinking, old habits, old ways of seeing the world and replaces them with the "new." Recall a few more biblical examples . . .

1. An army can't conquer the massive soldier on the other side of a river. God gives the army something new: a wiry teenager armed with just a sling and a few stones.

2. Egyptian battle chariots charge down upon the people of Israel in the desert. God gives them something new: a sea opens up and the Hebrews walk on dry land to the other shore.

3. A huge impenetrable wall fortifies a city. God gives His soldiers a new plan, a change in tactics: blow a horn and the walls will come tumbling down.

4. A man is executed for crimes he didn't commit. God gives the world something new: a risen Lord and Messiah.

5. One man is a tax collector, others are fishermen. God allows them to turn the world upside down by giving them something new to replace the old ways: the Good News of the Kingdom.

God gave me something new as well. I joined the team and have never looked back at the old way.

• *They followed immediately.* God only asks us to do one thing—follow immediately. That is what Matthew tells us. Jesus says, "Follow me" and (the King James Version says), "they straightaway left their nets." The Greek word *eutheos* is used for "straightaway," and it means "right now" or "immediately."

Then I heard the voice of the Lord saying, "Whom shall I send? And who will go for us?" And I said, "Here am I. Send me!"

—Isaiah 6:8 (NIV)

Oswald Chambers reminds us:

God doesn't single out someone and say, "Now, you go." He didn't force His will on Isaiah. Isaiah was in the presence of God, and he overheard the call. His response, performed in complete freedom, could only be to say, "Here am I! Send me."[2]

The person who delays when responsibility calls may never have it in his power to demonstrate the sincerity of his remorse for past folly and neglect. "I made haste," David said in Psalm 119:60, "and delayed not to keep thy commandments" (KJV). That is, being fully convinced of the necessity and excellency of obedience, he instantly resolved upon it, and immediately put it into execution.

You Can Form a "Family Team"

John Wooden, the legendary UCLA basketball coach once said, "Understanding that the good of the group comes first is fundamental to being a highly productive member of a team. It means being not just willing but eager to sacrifice personal interest or glory for the welfare of all."[3] Along those same lines, Rudyard Kipling wrote:

Now this is the law of the jungle—
As old and as true as the sky;
And the wolf that keep it may prosper,
But the wolf that shall break it must die.
As the creeper that girdles the tree trunk,
The law runneth forward and back—
And the strength of the pack is the wolf
And the strength of the wolf is the pack.

Joining and then creating a team is so very important at this point, or earlier, in the family cycle. What an incredible difference it made to our family for me to join the team! Now that I was on the team, we had to develop into a team. Great family teams are not born instantly. They develop over the years as their members employ biblical principles to fashion a group of people into a loving, fully functioning unit. Specifically, here's what it takes. . . .

• *Be willing to see others succeed.* The first quality of making a good family team is a willingness to see others succeed. The focus is upon others and their success in life. This goes beyond the quality of servant leadership; it's a strong desire to have our children (and our spouse) reach a high level of accomplishment in whatever they may do.

The Apostle Paul said it best, "I will very gladly spend and be spent for your souls" (2 Cor. 12:15, NKJV). He knew how to best build an effective team: simply enjoy the success of other people. This is truly a foundation for family success as well. Being a certified "sports nut," I naturally think of all the coaches I have admired—Vince Lombardi, Tom Landry, John Wooden, Walter Alston, Dean Smith, and Red Auerbach, for instance. These names speak of success in the development and leadership of winning teams. Each of these men had a simple formula for success. And each placed the success of their players ahead of their own personal achievement. They knew that the ultimate realization of a coach's goals depended upon his concern with making the players as successful as possible. Quoting Wooden again, "The main ingredient of stardom is the rest of the team."[4] Legendary Nebraska football coach Tom Osborne said, "At Nebraska, our coaching staff was encouraged to genuinely love and care about their players. . . . Each of them was expected to demonstrate an unconditional, positive regard toward the player's total well being."[5]

A multiplication effect kicks in when you work toward the success of your kids. Here the sum is greater than its parts. If you, as a parent, dedicate yourself to the success and fulfillment of the family, then this multiplication factor will begin to emerge. Family members will respond to your leadership with renewed dedication and energy as they sense your sensitivity to their needs. The more success you breed, the more success will blossom. Just keep elevating the needs of the "team" above your own.

• *Identify others' strengths, weaknesses, and needs.* We must understand each other fully in order to match our children's strengths with what they want to become or currently do. Jennifer was our actress and singer. She felt enlivened and exhilarated when standing in front of people (sometimes crowds), using her ability to communicate. Our family team best functioned when Jennifer was using this strength. We couldn't expect Jennifer to spend long, quiet hours reading or being still. She needed people, and we needed to help her to be in situations where she could exercise this strength. (This book will provide some tools for identifying a child's temperamental strengths and weaknesses in a later chapter.)

> *[14] As He passed by, He saw Levi the son of Alphaeus sitting at the tax office. And He said to him, "Follow Me." So he arose and followed Him.*
> *[15] Now it happened, as He was dining in Levi's house, that many tax collectors and sinners also sat together with Jesus and His disciples; for there were many, and they followed Him.*
> *[16] And when the scribes and Pharisees saw Him eating with the tax collectors and sinners, they said to His disciples, "How is it that He eats and drinks with tax collectors and sinners?"*
> *[17] When Jesus heard it, He said to them, "Those who are well have no need of a physician, but those who are sick. I didn't come to call the righteous, but sinners, to repentance."*
>
> —Mark 2:14-17 (NKJV)

Jesus formed the most important team ever assembled. This team would be charged with carrying on His ministry, teaching, and spreading the Good News. They would be the forefathers of the worldwide Christian church. The preceding passage recounts the calling of Matthew, and Jesus' response to criticism from the scribes and Pharisees. However, it also contains two very important lessons on team building.

First, Jesus knew the strengths and weaknesses of this team. He handpicked persons to do His work, and He needed special people who could do what was necessary to carry His message to the world. We can't handpick our children, but we can discern the specific areas where they excel, and we can guide them into those areas. Zachary showed an early bent toward music, so Pam found a music class for him at a very early age. We deliberately exposed him to areas of his interest; we highlighted specific strengths that he could build upon for lasting effect and positive well-being throughout his life.

Second, Jesus picked "odd" members for the team. He began with a group of Galileans (hard-working fishermen with strong Jewish backgrounds). Then He added Matthew, a tax collector, a hated publican, to the mix. Jesus worked with this team—knowing each member's strengths—and forged an efficient and effective evangelistic group (with only one failure, Judas).

You see, spouses add family members who are different from them. The process is called childbirth, and mixing genes from different families creates children who are quite different (temperamentally) from their parents. This is natural; it happens all the time. The important lesson is that we as parents not try to force our children to be just like us. We need to identify each child's strengths and weaknesses and work with each child to help him or her develop.

Let me provide one last comment on this point: *a person's weakness is usually a strength taken to its extreme.* Jennifer can perform or speak in front of crowds; she can easily talk to strangers and make them feel comfortable. Her weakness is that she can talk too much (her strength taken to its extreme). All of us have weaknesses; we just need to find a strength, take it to an extreme, and there it is! What does this tell you about your children at this point?

• *Establish a vision-setting environment in your family.* Peter Marshall prayed, "Give us clear vision that we may know where to stand and what to stand for, because unless we stand for something, we shall fall for anything."

Families need to know where they're going. Pam and I spent many hours discussing how we wanted our children raised, how we wanted to discipline them, how we wanted to help them be successful, and how we wanted to move them to adulthood. Vision helps us to see the end before we reach it. Vision is the lighthouse, standing strong and providing light even in the heaviest of fog (circumstances), high seas (criticism), and darkness (evil temptations).

Bowling is an enjoyable game, but would it be fun if there were no pins? Or suppose someone hung a sheet in front of the pins? We'd never know what we were aiming for. Or, would bowling be fun if, once we rolled the ball, we kept no score? I don't think so. Vision is much the same, giving us a clear target to aim for and providing a means to evaluate our efforts. The Book of Nehemiah is a wonderful accounting of a godly leader. Part of his success was his vision:

> [11] *I went to Jerusalem, and after staying there three days* [12] *I set out during the night with a few men. I had not told anyone what my God had put in my heart to do for Jerusalem. There were no mounts with me except the one I was riding on.*
> [13] *By night I went out through the Valley Gate toward the Jackal Well and the Dung Gate, examining the walls of Jerusalem, which had been broken down, and its gates, which had been destroyed by fire.*
> [14] *Then I moved on toward the Fountain Gate and the*

King's Pool, but there was not enough room for my mount to get through;
¹⁵ so I went up the valley by night, examining the wall. Finally, I turned back and reentered through the Valley Gate.
¹⁶ The officials did not know where I had gone or what I was doing, because as yet I had said nothing to the Jews or the priests or nobles or officials or any others who would be doing the work.
¹⁷ Then I said to them, "You see the trouble we are in: Jerusalem lies in ruins, and its gates have been burned with fire. Come, let us rebuild the wall of Jerusalem, and we will no longer be in disgrace."
¹⁸ I also told them about the gracious hand of my God upon me and what the king had said to me. They replied, "Let us start rebuilding." So they began this good work.

—Nehemiah 2:11-18 (NIV)

Nehemiah was looking to God for an answer. He had seen the need, and now in solitude he was looking for a vision and an answer to his problem. Before launching into this tremendous project, Nehemiah decides to listen first to God.

After he heard from God, Nehemiah inspected the area. The biblical word used for "inspect" is the same word used to describe a doctor probing a wound to see the extent of the damage. Nehemiah probed, and then he decided to plan it all out.

In verse 17, notice that Nehemiah used the words "us" and "we." He did not stand back and throw criticism at the people, telling them what they should do. Instead, Nehemiah became part of the solution and identified himself with the problem. In other words, Nehemiah decided to join the team.

Then Nehemiah motivated the people. He decided not to use materialistic motivation, though. You know how this *doesn't* work at home: "Honey, will you clean up your room?

I'll give you $5 if you clean it up today." This type of motivation usually doesn't work with children, and it wouldn't have worked with Nehemiah's people. Instead, this visionary painted the future for them and appealed to their intrinsic needs. Nehemiah knew how to create a vision:

he checked with God;
he planned ahead;
he included the team;
he painted the vision;
he focused on God.

When we set the vision, then each family member can have a fun part in charting the future. Setting vision can help us steer the family ship in the right direction, showing us any need for mid-course corrections. Jennifer, as a child, wanted to be a ballet dancer, and then she wanted to be a professional singer, then a Broadway star or Oprah Winfrey. Each step of the way she had a vision. We helped her (putting her in areas of her strength to help her learn about her vision), and she came to realize the best goals for her. Each step of the way, however, we stayed focused on guidance from God while we planned together.

Plan for Learning, Learning, Learning

Every minute we are with our children is an opportunity to teach them. The family team will function well if the members take time to learn and teach. I'm not talking about formal sessions here, of course. Simply looking at the sky can be a big lesson in God's creation. Your teaching just needs to be consistent and from the heart. As you seek to be the best teacher you can be in your family, keep these qualities of effective teaching in mind, all of which are based on biblical examples. . . .

• *Effective teaching is a continual necessity.* This is the case because the truth is always one generation away from extinction!

[10] After that generation died, another generation grew up who did not acknowledge the LORD or remember the mighty things he had done for Israel.
[11] Then the Israelites did what was evil in the Lord's sight and worshiped the images of Baal.
[12] They abandoned the LORD, the God of their ancestors, who had brought them out of Egypt. They chased after other gods, worshiping the gods of the people around them. And they angered the LORD.
[13] They abandoned the LORD to serve Baal and the images of Ashtoreth.

—Judges 2:10-13 (NLT)

This passage is a brief preview of the cycle of sin, judgment, and repentance that Israel experienced repeatedly. Each generation failed to convey to the next generation all that God had done—and all the worship God deserved.

• *Effective teaching relates truth to life.*

[1] These are all the commands, laws, and regulations that the LORD your God told me to teach you so you may obey them in the land you are about to enter and occupy,
[2] and so you and your children and grandchildren might fear the LORD your God as long as you live. If you obey all his laws and commands, you will enjoy a long life.
[3] Listen closely, Israel, to everything I say. Be careful to obey. Then all will go well with you, and you will have many children in the land flowing with milk and honey, just as the LORD, the God of your ancestors, promised you.
[4] Hear, O Israel! The LORD is our God, the LORD alone.
[5] And you must love the LORD your God with all your heart, all your soul, and all your strength.

*6 And you must commit yourselves wholeheartedly to
these commands I am giving you today.*
—Deuteronomy 6:1-6 (NLT)

I like the way Tyndale's *Handbook of Bible Application*
comments on this passage, so I'll let it do the talking under this
heading:

*The Hebrews were extremely successful at making reli-
gion an integral part of life. The reason for their success
was that religious education was life-oriented, not
information-oriented. They used the context of daily life
to teach about God. The key to teaching your children
to love God is stated simply and clearly in these verses.
If you want your children to follow God, you must make
God a part of your everyday experiences. You must
teach your children diligently to see God in all aspects
of life, not just those that are church related.[6]*

• *Effective teaching can occur anywhere, anyplace.* In our
family, some of our best teaching times arose during normal,
everyday situations. Many times a ride to school or the sharing
of a cool drink on a warm day provided wonderful opportunities to teach our children about God and His world. The
Hebrews made a point of making sure that God's Word was on
their doorposts, and this gave the parents plenty of opportunities to teach their children how to love God as well as love
their neighbors.

•*Effective teaching is the responsibility of every Christian.*
Noted speaker Ken Blanchard once wrote, "I thought those people I hired had certain training. I assumed they came into the office
knowing what they were supposed to do. I didn't realize that I had
to help them develop their skills."[7] Don't many parents make the
same assumption? We assume the church or the Christian school is
teaching our children all they need to know. Yet we Christian parents must take full responsibility for teaching our children about
God and His commandments. It will make a better family team if

we all know and understand the wonderful, freeing truth of faith in Jesus Christ.

• *Effective teaching means tailoring your style to each person.* "People need a manager who understands their needs, and then provides them with the type of support necessary to achieve their goals."[8] Later in this book, we'll spend a great deal of time on temperaments and how to know our children and ourselves. The family team is comprised of several temperaments, and it functions best when we can modify our personal style to meet each child's unique needs.

Jennifer was a talker who enjoyed people and being with people. She also didn't like detail. Therefore, when we were working with Jennifer, we couldn't offer all the details, or expect accuracy in all the details she gave us. Instead, we had to go straight to the main point, almost shocking her into listening. Details would have bored her, but shooting straight to the "bottom line" of the issue helped us successfully parent her in discipline-type situations.

• *A constant flow of feedback.* The trick is to catch your children doing something right. It doesn't help to focus only on what they're doing wrong. The better way is to highlight those times when our children really exceed our expectations.

[1] One day Jesus called together his twelve apostles and gave them power and authority to cast out demons and to heal all diseases.

[2] Then he sent them out to tell everyone about the coming of the Kingdom of God and to heal the sick.

[3] "Don't even take along a walking stick," he instructed them, "nor a traveler's bag, nor food, nor money. Not even an extra coat.

[4] When you enter each village, be a guest in only one home.

[5] If the people of the village won't receive your message when you enter it, shake off its dust from your feet as

you leave. It is a sign that you have abandoned that village to its fate."
⁶ So they began their circuit of the villages, preaching the Good News and healing the sick.
¹⁰ When the apostles returned, they told Jesus everything they had done. Then he slipped quietly away with them toward the town of Bethsaida.

—Luke 9:1-6, 10 (NLT)

These few verses show the Master and His model for great team management. The important message for us parents comes in verse 10. Notice that Jesus listened to everything they had done (seeking feedback), and then He took them away to a quiet place. Not to add to Scripture, but I'd like to think that Jesus led them away to a quiet place *in order to help them.* He must have wanted to get alone with them in order to counsel with them. He no doubt wanted to take time to praise and correct them.

When the twelve had finished their mission, they returned and told their Master all that they had done and taught. Of their report, or of His remarks thereon, no details are recorded. Such details we do find, however, in connection with the later mission of the seventy. "The seventy," we read, "returned again with joy, saying, Lord, even the devils are subject unto us through Thy name." The same evangelist from whom these words are quoted, informs us that, after congratulating the disciples on their success, and expressing His own satisfaction with the facts reported, Jesus spoke to them the warning word: "Notwithstanding in this rejoice not, that the spirits are subject unto you; but rather rejoice because your names are written in heaven."⁹

It takes time to catch our kids doing things right. We can't expect to do it by just sitting on the parenting "sidelines." We must make a commitment to be involved; we must join the team, and we must help our kids understand that when they choose to do the right thing—making good life choices—we will be there to offer positive encouragement and praise.

This constant flow of feedback also helps us begin to help our children be accountable. Only by listening and seeking feedback can we ever expect to help our children know right from wrong choices. Only feedback can help us train them in the importance of personal accountability for their actions.

Don't Be a Seagull Parent!

We live near the Pacific Ocean, and we love to take walks along Pismo Beach and on the Pismo pier. The area is beautiful and, like most beach areas, full of seagulls. Seagulls are interesting to watch as they fly around looking for scraps of food or recently caught fish on the pier or shoreline.

Nice, but you don't want to be a seagull parent. Seagull parents just swoop in, looking for the scraps. Seagull parents not only just swoop in, they usually leave a mess and then swoop back out again! The mess in this case may be emotional, or simply hurt feelings because the child, like Jesus' disciples, just wanted to talk about the circumstances of their triumphs and defeats.

Seagull parents subtract from their kids instead of adding to them. When they whoosh in and "dump" they've made a choice to take rather than give. The word "curse" in the Scriptures usually refers to a dried-up stream because water has been subtracted from it. As seagull parents, we choose to subtract from our kids rather than having the courage to let them draw nourishment, strength, and emotional support from us. I know it's difficult; sometimes we feel so depleted ourselves. But just spending time with them and listening is half the battle. Good parents bless their children with eye contact, appropriate touch, reflective listening, and positive words.

Once you join the team, there is no turning back. When Pam encouraged me to join the ranks and help build the team, it was a life-changing, as well as family-changing step. We have been a team for a long time, and we've never regretted that choice.

I started small. After Pam's admonition, I began to give Jennifer her nightly bath. She was so used to her mother doing this for her, that it took a few nights to "wean" her away from that routine. However, over time, it became a ritual for her. In the next chapter I'll explain how this simple event went to the next level in raising her. However, for now I just want to say that the benefits of joining are tremendous. So, if you haven't already . . . please join the ranks!

Notes

1 *The Victor Bible Background Commentary,* New Testament, "The Calling of the First Disciples" (Colorado Springs: Cook Communications, Inc., 1994).

2 Oswald Chambers, *My Utmost for His Highest,* "Called by God" © 1992 by Oswald Chambers Publications Association, Ltd. United States publication rights are held by Discovery House Publishers, which is affiliated with RBC Ministries, Grand Rapids, Michigan 49512. Electronic Edition STEP Files © 1998, Parsons Technology, Inc.

3 Quote taken from: Jim Sheard & James F. Gauss, *A Champion's Heart, Qualities for Success in Life and Sport* (Nashville: Thomas Nelson, 1999), pp. 112-113.

4 John Wooden, *They Call Me Coach* (Chicago: NTC Publishing Group, 1988.), p. 106.

5 Tom Osborne, *Faith in the Game* (Colorado Springs: WaterBrook Press, 1999), p. 129.

6 *The Handbook of Bible Application* (Wheaton, IL: Tyndale House, 1992), electronic edition.

7 Ken Blanchard, "Organization Size Does Not Determine Management Style," *Personal Selling Power,* March 1989, p. 19.

8 Ibid.

9 *The Training of the Twelve,* Public Domain. Electronic Edition, STEP Files © 1997, Parsons Technology, Inc.

THE ELEMENTARY YEARS – A TIME TO PLAY

℞

Chapter 3

THE ELEMENTARY OR PRIMARY SCHOOL YEARS are times of explosive change in our children. Children usually go to elementary school between six and twelve years of age. This is when they build on, and improve, their previously learned skills. They begin to make friends and become more interested in the world around them.

Children at this age are becoming independent. They enjoy responsibilities and challenges that they can manage. Conversely, they get frustrated with challenges and responsibilities that are out of their reach or that they are incapable of completing.

Their social skills are improving. Children in the elementary years often enjoy playing in small groups of three or four children. They learn concepts like sharing, speaking in turn, and other aspects of group dynamics. Their physical skills are also improving. They may be interested in several kinds of activity. With increased coordination, playing sports, listening to music, and participating in other activities become important parts of their lives.

They begin to develop hobbies and special interests and learn a lot from such activities. Scouting and other clubs are important, as kids at this age mix the social interaction with physical games and special interests.

During these years, the sound of my daughter's voice was one of laughter. Jennifer had (and thankfully still has) a wonderful lilting laugh. She spent lots of her time in social situations, and she always laughed easily. The sparkle in her eye, and the sense of humor she developed in these years, has helped her through many tough situations later in life.

Dad the Playmate

Our relationship really flourished during this period. As Jennifer grew older, we began to reserve large chunks of time in the evenings and on my day off to just spend time playing and laughing together.

As I mentioned in the previous chapter, playing started with Jennifer's bath time. She was so used to her mother, that it took a little time for her to get used to me being involved. However, once we broke that barrier down, we enjoyed every night together. These simple, early moments built a sound foundation for the future. Bath time gave us a way to have fun with each other, learn about each other, and just laugh with each other in a safe and nonthreatening environment. It gave us freedom to be ourselves and learn how to make each other relax and just enjoy the moment.

As Jennifer grew from a toddler, we began to spend time together with books. I'll never forget those days of having her cuddle in my lap or sit next to me on the couch as I read to her. Parents should never underestimate the marvelous time they can share with their children by just reading books to them. Jennifer and I shared so many adventures with her books. As she grew older, she could begin reading some of the words. Then, later, she began reading aloud to the whole family. This not only helped advance her reading skills, it gave her yet another "stage" on which she could perform—an important part of her temperament and an easy way for us to put her in an area of strength.

Looking back, we can still reminisce about the lessons learned and the characters we shared together. From Ferdinand the Bull to Laura Ingalls Wilder, Jennifer immensely enjoyed our reading times together. And they gave me not only a score of memories, but provided opportunity for me to be a teaching dad.

We weren't always reading, though! Jennifer and I also spent a significant amount of time just playing together. Dad, have you considered learning how to be a kid again? Or is it just a matter of letting our "child side" come out a bit more? In our case, usually after dinner, we would retreat to her bedroom and it would be transformed to a unique place limited only by Jennifer's imagination. Pam had given Jennifer many old clothes to use as toys, and Jennifer used them to create unique characters and moments. I think her favorite game was "restaurant." Jennifer would dress up and serve me tea and cookies. I made certain I was on the floor with her, acting my part as the customer, while she played music and treated me to all the other fineries of her imaginary restaurant.

As Jennifer grew, we continued to enjoy times of play. Playing board games, enjoying backyard baseball, and doing all kinds of other activities helped us to form a strong father-daughter relationship. Not only were we spending time focusing on an activity, the activity itself usually gave us the opportunity to learn how to react to each other and communicate with each other. These times were special and helped Jennifer form her sense of self and her sense of humor.

Clearly, playing with your children gives you some unique ways to help them develop and grow. Assuming you may not be totally convinced, in this chapter, I'd like to focus on four developmental areas that playing strengthens: it gives the parent time to offer encouragement; it helps a child gain confidence; it increases a child's self-esteem; and it creates a special, lasting bond of love.

Playing Conveys Encouragement

Playing with Jennifer gave me a real opportunity to encourage her into many positive areas of growth. As we played together, I could see where Jennifer had strengths and where she needed personal development. I could then fashion games or situations that would help me to guide and teach her along those lines.

Jennifer was always musical. Our playing together most always included some kind of song or performance. In this way, Jennifer could be free to exercise her passion to entertain and sing, yet she had a very warm, friendly audience. This experience translated itself into reality when at five, Jennifer sang her first solo in my praise and worship band. She had to stand on a chair to reach the microphone, but nonetheless, she belted out her part of the song in unwavering confidence. That was her first of many solos before a large audience. I don't think she'd have had the same poise or confidence had I not given her tons of encouraging words in our play times together.

An old proverb says, "More people fail for lack of encouragement than for any other reason." [1] We parents need to learn this! Failing to encourage our children is something that will lead them onto a path of personal failure and lack of confidence. Encouragement requires words, and these special words are pointed to help our children grow and be the people God wants them to be.

Encouraging words are often instructional words, as well. In the Bible, we see that the Apostle Paul found it necessary to encourage and teach his new leadership team. His letter to Titus is a good example of this.

[1] You must teach what is in accord with sound doctrine.
[2] Teach the older men to be temperate, worthy of respect, self-controlled, and sound in faith, in love and in endurance.
[3] Likewise, teach the older women to be reverent in the way they live, not to be slanderers or addicted to much wine, but to teach what is good.
[4] Then they can train the younger women to love their husbands and children,

5 to be self-controlled and pure, to be busy at home, to be kind, and to be subject to their husbands, so that no one will malign the word of God.
6 Similarly, encourage the young men to be self-controlled.
7 In everything set them an example by doing what is good. In your teaching show integrity, seriousness
8 and soundness of speech that cannot be condemned, so that those who oppose you may be ashamed because they have nothing bad to say about us.
9 Teach slaves to be subject to their masters in everything, to try to please them, not to talk back to them,
10 and not to steal from them, but to show that they can be fully trusted, so that in every way they will make the teaching about God our Savior attractive.
11 For the grace of God that brings salvation has appeared to all men.
12 It teaches us to say "No" to ungodliness and worldly passions, and to live self-controlled, upright and godly lives in this present age,
13 while we wait for the blessed hope—the glorious appearing of our great God and Savior, Jesus Christ,
14 who gave himself for us to redeem us from all wickedness and to purify for himself a people that are his very own, eager to do what is good.
15 These, then, are the things you should teach. Encourage and rebuke with all authority. Do not let anyone despise you.

—Titus 2:1-15 (NIV)

When we integrate the terms and concepts of this passage into our parenting task of encouragement, what do we discover? I'd like to highlight at least seven valuable insights—

First, "teach" sound doctrine is from the Greek word *laleo*, "to speak, assert, proclaim." The subject of this vocal teaching isn't "sound doctrine" itself, but a lifestyle that is in harmony with the revealed truths that shape our understanding of God and of the meaning of life in this world. Yes, Paul wants his leaders to follow scriptural truth, but he wants more than that for them—he wants them to develop a worldview consistent with God's Word. As we encourage certain behavior from our children, our encouragement should likewise help them develop a worldview centered upon God's Word.

Second, in verse 3, the women are told to "teach what is good." The Greek word used here is *kalodidaskalous*, and it is used only here in the New Testament. The word is actually two words glued together. The first means "honorable" and the second means "teacher" "or doctor." The older women are responsible themselves to be admirable persons (or persons with honor), and then to instruct the younger women. They are to encourage behavior that is God-centered and that they have learned from their own experience to be the right way.

Third, Paul calls Titus to train. "Train" here is the Greek *sophrontizo*. It means "to encourage, advise, urge." In New Testament times, the word focused on teaching morality and good judgment. In essence, the older women were to show concern for the moral development and improvement of the younger women. We, as parents, should always focus our encouragement on that same concern. In fact, the more we focus on development and improvement, the more secure our children will feel and become.

Fourth, in verse 6, Paul tells Titus to encourage. "Encourage" is *parakaleo,* which means "to encourage or exhort." It suggests a close relationship; a closeness allowing one man to correct a younger man. Playtime was one way for me to develop a unique closeness with Jennifer that allowed me to positively correct and advise her. It gave us a contact that I don't believe we would have developed if we hadn't spent hours down on the floor simply playing and having fun. Later, as she grew into her teens, this intimate foundation made it possible for me to approach Jennifer and counsel her when, in many cases, she may not have wanted to listen to me. Our early experience had taught her to trust me; she knew that my ultimate goal was always to encourage and develop her. She knew my motive was to help her be a better person.

Fifth, verse 7 speaks of setting an example. "Example" translates the Greek word *typon*. This word means more than "a visible impression." It suggests "a pattern to follow." We teach others God's ways by showing them our way of life. Years ago there was an anti-smoking commercial on television. It showed a father walking along, and behind him was his son. When the father picked up a rock and threw it, so did the little boy. The father looked approvingly at nature; so did the little boy. Then the father sits down to have a smoke. The next scene shows the little boy looking longingly at the cigarettes. The tag line is: "Like Father, like son." The commercial dramatizes exactly what our children do when they see us in action, and it is exactly what the Greek word *typon* is saying in Titus 2. Like it or not, parents set the example for their children by their own behaviors. If our words are always discouraging, then our children will be discouraged.

Sixth, in verse 12, "teaches" (Titus 2:12) translates the Greek *paideuousa*. The word suggests giving parent-like guidance and daily correction, as to a child. Providing encouragement through teaching is a daily activity for parents. We need to find every opportunity to teach, encourage, and train our children.

Finally, "reprove" in Titus 2:15 is *elencho*, which means, "to bring to light, expose." In context, it means to convince, to reprove if necessary, in order to convict. I believe we can add light to our children's behavior by encouraging them through reproof. When we shed light on our children's behavior (especially positive behavior) we help them see the right way to respond in life situations.

So there you have it: Encouraging our children (through taking time to teach them while we play) is a task of shaping their lives, not simply of passing on true information. It involves every aspect of their lives. The tensions of daily life, relationships with others—all these things are the concerns on which parental encouragement and teaching should focus. Thus encouragement means bringing the insights of Scripture to bear on the whole child through modeling, instructing, encouraging, advising, urging, exhorting, guiding, and convicting.

Playing Builds Confidence

More than a decade of research shows that children who feel confident that they can master an assignment—like learning to write the letters of the alphabet—will try harder, stick with it longer, and ultimately accomplish the task they set out to do. They will try more tasks, as well.

The formula for confidence building is straightforward: Success raises confidence, failure lowers it. "Parents should try to structure learning situations to bring success and avoid placing children in situations in which they are sure to fail," says Dr. Albert Bandura, a professor of psychology at Stanford University. He goes on to add, "The more competent the child feels, the harder he will try, the longer he will persevere in the face of obstacles, and the quicker he will bounce back after failure." [2]

As Jennifer and I played, I made it a point to allow her to be the one to build confidence. Not only was I encouraging to her, but our games and times of play allowed her to feel special and to grow in her personal confidence. I found it to be a delicate balance between simple flattery and confidence-building praise. I had to make certain that she was actually *performing* challenging, yet doable tasks. If I simply gave her *empty* praise, she could see right through that! In that case, I defeated all I had done or was trying to do for her by my simple sweet talk. Barry Zimmerman, Ph.D., a professor of educational psychology at the City University of New York, writes:

Some kids, battered by failure, need help finding successes to feel good about. Otherwise, there can be a downward spiral and they give up when they don't see results. To perceive improvement, they need help setting goals and keeping track of their progress. [3]

Second Corinthians 4 and 5 explain much to us about building confidence. There Paul's confident reassurance of the Corinthians was not an attempt to manipulate them. It was not just a motivational technique. Instead, what Paul was doing was sharing with these uncertain and ashamed believers what he really felt about them. As we build our children's confidence, so too must our words be truly what we feel about them (often based on what we observe in their behavior), not used merely to flatter or manipulate.

Expressions of confidence, if honest, do motivate. However, such expressions cannot initially be based on a child's past performance. If our hope for ourselves and for others is based on performance, there is bound to be a growing sense of discouragement, and ultimately, the loss of hope. Yet this is a trap that parents often fall into with their children. Time after time, they instruct, encourage, or request. In addition, time after time the child fails to respond, or "forgets," or simply ignores. He doesn't do his homework. She forgets to make her bed. He neglects his chores. Before long, this wears away a parent's patience. And before long, the parent *expects* the child to disappoint! Moreover, the child, sensing the parent's attitude, begins to expect himself or herself to fail. He or she loses self-confidence and any hope of personal success.

The child learns to live by the expectations of failure that we may have communicated, however subtly. It is, therefore, so important for us to learn Paul's secret. The secret tells of maintaining one's own confidence, and thus being able to build confidence and hope—and the motivation to change—into others' lives. What is the secret? Paul explained, "We do not lose heart" (2 Cor. 4:1). Paul was deeply aware that God had entrusted him with his ministry. As to the Gospel message, God is able to make its light shine in dark hearts. Ultimately, God is the source of all change in human hearts (2 Cor. 4:1-6). This is a key concept for parents to absorb. It seems so easy for many of us to lose heart, yet it is also the work of the enemy, and we must battle it through prayer and being in His Word daily.

As for Paul himself, he was deeply aware that he was a mere "jar of clay." Despite the terrible pressures under which he must have lived (see 2 Cor. 4:7-12), Paul spoke out with faith and confidence. He knew that "the one who raised the Lord Jesus from the dead will also raise us with Jesus and present us with you in his presence" (2 Cor. 4:14). The message of Christ glows with a vitalizing power, the very power that raised Jesus from the dead, the power at work in all who trust Him. Often our parenting tanks are running on empty and we need to accept the power that Christ offers us.

"Therefore," Paul said, "we do not lose heart" (2 Cor. 4:16). The foundation for Paul's confidence in the Corinthians was his bedrock belief in Jesus, and the resurrection power that the message of Jesus unleashes. He reminds us again of Christ's available power to help us and then for us to move ahead offering encouragement and building confidence in our children.

At this point Paul laid down an important principle that was at the core of his confidence. Outwardly, Paul admitted deterioration: we are "wasting away." However, inwardly Paul experienced a daily renewal. As a result, Paul said, "We fix our eyes not on what is seen, but on what is unseen. For what is seen is temporary, but what is unseen is eternal" (2 Cor. 4:18).

This concept deserves exploration. What Paul said is that anything that exists in this world of time and space is subject to change. Children grow up. Job descriptions change. Buildings decay. Civilizations fall. Wind and rain can erode even the mightiest cliffs. Anything that we can see is by its very nature subject to change.

This is true of those children of ours who cannot

remember to make their beds, and of the Corinthians, who couldn't seem to get beyond disputes and arguments. If what troubles us is a behavior that we can see, then we need to remember that it is temporary. It will change, by the very nature of things in this world of change. How foolish, then, to become discouraged and give up, even if behavior that bothers us persists for months or years. We need to remember, with Paul, that what we see can change. We need to remember that we can transfer this confidence to our children (and through them gaining that confidence, things *will* change).

As we work with our children (through play or other means), we not only need to remember that some things are temporary, but we must also fix our hope on unseen things that are eternal. This "fixing of our gaze" will help us teach our children a confidence in the eternal as well. This type of confidence will then translate to their daily behavior and help them in everyday situations.

Many parents make the mistake of losing patience and then putting lifelong labels on their kids. For example, Johnny, during a certain stage of his life, is loud and boisterous. Dad loses patience and labels Johnny a "loud mouth" instead of using encouragement to move his son toward the next stage of maturity. Chances are high that Johnny will never lose that early label and it will act as a self-fulfilling prophecy in Johnny's adult life.

Paul pointed out that it is only appropriate that we live by the heartbeat of God's life rather than by the old heartbeat of humankind. Since Jesus loved and died for believers, they should "no longer live for themselves but for him who died for them and was raised again" (2 Cor. 5:15). As they do this, they will "become the righteousness of God" in Him (2 Cor. 5:21).

It is this goal of leading believers to life in full harmony with God's righteousness that Paul had in mind when he said, "We implore you on Christ's behalf: Be reconciled to God" (2 Cor. 5:20). With this understood, we can go back and look at Paul's explanation of how he could express such amazing confidence even in the carnal Corinthians. Paul began the paragraph assuring the Corinthians that his expressions of confidence were no insincere attempt at flattery (2 Cor. 5:11-12). Yet, how could Paul be completely honest and, while criticizing the Corinthians' behavior, still speak of his joy and confidence in their future progress? Paul explained that this was because his approach was so different from "those who take pride in what is seen rather than what is in the heart" (2 Cor. 5:12).

This statement takes us back to the core concept expressed earlier. Some people incorrectly base their pride on what can be seen and measured. "Aren't the folks in my congregation spiritual! Fifty percent of them show up on prayer-meeting night." And, "My Jimmy is an ideal Christian boy. Why, he reads his Bible every day."

This isn't to say we shouldn't be pleased by evidence of spiritual progress or commitment. But pride in the 50 percent who come means shame on the 50 percent who don't! And, neither coming nor not coming provides a basis for judgment of individual spiritual progress. Indeed, because anything that can be seen is temporary and subject to change, those who boast in externals set themselves up for a fall when the percentage drops off, or Jimmy forsakes his Bible reading.

In what, then, are we to take pride? Paul answers, "What is in the heart." We can't see what is in the heart, of course. We can't measure it. However, the Christian knows that Jesus Himself is resident in the heart of believers. And Jesus is eternal; He won't change, no matter what. Paul told the Corinthians his view wasn't madness (2 Cor. 5:13). It was utter sanity. Because, Paul said, "Christ's love compels us" (2 Cor. 5:14).

Paul's point was this: Only one thing will bring about change in a believer's life and move him or her toward Christlikeness. Christ Himself pours that love into the heart in which He dwells. Mere human forms of motivation—attempts to coerce, to shame, to move by guilt—may bring conformity of action. *But they will never change the heart, and it is the heart—the unseen world within—with which parents should be concerned.* [4]

Building children's confidence means transferring the assurance we have in Christ to them. It means that we are building them to be more Christlike with a strong confidence that is based, not on personal achievement, but upon a heart supported by Christ's work on the cross.

Carol Dweck, Ph.D., a professor of psychology at Columbia University in New York City, has studied these things for more than two decades. Her research with thousands of kids, age three and up, suggests that if a child thinks she can get smarter, she achieves more.[5] Building confidence is a tool to help the child see her true image in God's eyes and understand that she can change. The Apostle Paul, in 2 Corinthians, reminds us of the same kind of life-changing belief as we trust Christ and communicate His risen power and glory to our children. That will serve to build their confidence in the "internals."

Playing Develops Self-Esteem

"Being a parent is about the hardest job in the world, and at times every mother and father feels insecure and inadequate," says Tom Olkowski, Ph.D., a clinical psychologist in Denver, Colorado, who runs self-esteem workshops. But when you let your children know you think you're inept, unattractive, or just not smart enough, you're sending them the message that you have low self-esteem. And that can affect the way your children think about themselves, says Linda Dunlap, Ph.D., an early-childhood specialist and chair of the Department of Psychology at Marist College in Poughkeepsie, New York. "Kids whose parents have a negative self-image have a more difficult time feeling positive about themselves," she says. [6]

John 10:10 says, "The thief comes only to steal, and kill, and destroy; I came that they might have life, and might have it abundantly" (NASB). Jesus does not want us to have a life that is empty and without positive feelings about ourselves. The

King James Version of this passage calls us to an abundant life. But how can we live an abundant life, or help our children to live this lifestyle if we don't take the time to help them build their self-esteem?

Kevin Leman, in his book *Becoming the Parent God Wants You to Be,* looks closely at the characteristics of self-esteem. He points out that there can be a healthy balance of helping our children feel loved, secure, accepted, etc., *without* raising a selfish child. Truly, balance is important. However, our self-image (how we picture ourselves) is a vitally important aspect of good parenting.

Dr. Leman provides a study of self-image and Jesus' relationship with His father. The table [7] below shows the necessary balance and scriptural truth of a positive self-image and self-esteem.

Jesus knew He was loved by His Father.	Matthew 3:17; 17:5
Jesus could love others because He was secure in the love of His Father.	John 15:9
Jesus' relationship with His Father gave Him purpose in life.	Luke 2:48-50
Jesus was affirmed by His Father.	Matthew 3:17; 17:5
Jesus was secure in His identity.	Matthew 16:13-20 John 10:24-30; 13:13
Jesus' positive sense of self allowed Him to withstand criticism.	Matthew 26:6-10
Jesus' positive sense of self allowed Him to relate to those less fortunate, rather than building His image by relating only to the rich and powerful.	Mark 2:15-17
Jesus knew He belonged to His Father.	John 10:30; 17:21
Jesus felt competent and equipped by His Father to do what He needed to do.	Matthew 28:18

When I consider your heavens, the work of your fingers, the moon and the stars, which you have set in place, what is man that you are mindful of him, the son of man that you care for him?

—Psalm 8:3-4 (NIV)

The next time you question your worth as a person, remember that God considers you highly valuable. The next time you consider the worth of your children, remember that God considers them highly valuable, and they should be made aware of that at every opportunity. We have great worth because we bear the stamp of the Creator. (See Genesis 1:26-27 for the extent of worth God places on all people.) Because God has already declared how valuable we are to Him, we can be set free from feelings of worthlessness and can set our children free as well. A good self-image is grounded in the value God places on our lives.

For by the grace given me I say to every one of you: Do not think of yourself more highly than you ought, but rather think of yourself with sober judgment, in accordance with the measure of faith God has given you.

—Romans 12:3 (NIV)

Healthy self-esteem is important because some of us think too little of ourselves; on the other hand, some of us overestimate ourselves. The key to an honest and accurate evaluation is knowing the basis of our worth—our identity in Christ. Apart from Him, we aren't capable of very much by eternal standards; in Him, we are valuable and capable of worthy service. Letting your children evaluate themselves by the worldly standards of success and achievement can cause them to think too much about their worth in the eyes of others and thus fail to spot their true value in God's eyes. So remember: Our self-esteem is affected by how closely we identify with Christ.

The time I spent with Jennifer in playful activities helped me develop and build her self-esteem and self-image. It gave me the opportunity to point her in the right direction and help her understand that Christ is the basis for any evaluation of her personal worth. This "education" for Jennifer became an important gift from me to her.

Many parents fail to give a critically important gift to their children. If you fail to give this gift, two things happen, both bad. First, your children will be vulnerable and unprotected as they grow up. They will be susceptible to the negative influences of the world. And we have plenty of negative influences, don't we? Second, as adults, your children will be limited in many ways. The lack of this gift affects your children well into adulthood.

If you succeed in giving this gift, two things happen, both good. First, your children will be protected as they grow up. They will have a fighting chance against the world's attacks. I should say, Satan's attacks, because he's in charge of the world (see 1 John 5:19). You can't change Satan or the world, but you can give something to your kids to help them in the fight. Second, you can provide your kids with a healthy foundation for the rest of their lives.

The gift I'm talking about is healthy self-esteem. One of your most important jobs as a parent is to be actively building the self-esteem of your children. This is second only to bringing your children to Christ and nurturing them spiritually.[8] Self-esteem grows as children are given the opportunity to accomplish tasks while proving themselves responsible and accountable.

Playing Creates an Unbreakable Bond

The new "super glues" are incredibly effective bonding agents. A person only has to get some on his fingers to fully understand how well these glues work. Believe me, it's no fun trying to get those fingers separated!

From what I understand, super glues actually melt the two items together to create an unbreakable bond. They aren't just topical substances; they get inside the elements, break them down, and then join them forever.

That is what I believe playing has done for Jennifer and me

(and it applied to Zachary as well). We have a "super glue" type of bond between us. Playing was the catalyst to break down barriers; laughter was an agent for change and encouragement; confidence and increased self-esteem building were the end results. Specifically . . .

• *It joined us.* Just like our fantastic modern glues, playing created a virtually indestructible bond between Jennifer and me. Today we are very close, and we know and understand each other well. I don't think we would have achieved this closeness without the hours we spent just playing together. Jennifer has seen me be crazy, laugh, and play like a kid. I was able to watch Jennifer interact in various situations and, from that, form plans for helping her interact even better with people. We have spent countless hours just sitting on the floor in silly situations. She was not just a little kid, and I was not just the disciplinarian. We enjoyed hours upon hours of fun, together.

• *It strengthened us.* I realize this sounds funny, but Jennifer and I have competed against one another, we have sharpened each other, and we have counseled each other. Jennifer and Zachary are important people in my life, and I think it all starts with trust. I really do trust my kids. Playing together gave us a mutual bond that developed later in life into a trusting relationship. Out of all that silliness and competition came a strong sense of "iron sharpening iron." We trust each other and we confide in each other. I seek Jennifer's help, and she regularly seeks mine. Only a close relationship, an open relationship, and a relationship that encouraged playing together would allow us to be so strong in helping each other.

• *It united us in love.* In Colossians 3, Paul lists a number of Christian attributes. He then says, "And over all these virtues put on love, which binds them all together in perfect unity" (v. 14 NIV). Warren Wiersbe writes:

Put on . . . love (Col. 3:14). This is the most important

of the Christian virtues, and it acts like a "girdle" that ties all the other virtues together. All of the spiritual qualities Paul has named are aspects of true Christian love, as a reading of 1 Corinthians 13 will reveal. Love is the first of the fruit of the Spirit and the other virtues follow—joy (Col. 3:16), peace (Col. 3:15), long-suffering, gentleness, kindness, and meekness (Col. 3:12). [9]

Love did act as a "girdle" around Jennifer and me as we played and learned from each other. The virtue kept us laughing and it kept Jennifer learning from the experience of just playing games and having fun times with her father. The girdle allowed me to affect Jennifer's life with Christlike teaching about her self-worth and gave her great confidence, a real "can do" attitude. How is it with you and your child today?

Notes

1 Edythe Draper, *Draper's Book of Quotations for the Christian World,* # 3138.

2 Liz Rusch, "Child Confidence = Success," September, 1998, www.parents.com; Gruner + Jahr USA Publishing.

3 Ibid.

4 Some of this Bible study on 2 Corinthians was taken from *The Teacher's Commentary* by Lawrence O. Richards (Colorado Springs: Cook Communications).

5 Liz Rusch, Op. cit.

6 Carolyn Hoyt, "Like Parent, Like Child," (CTW Family Workshop).

7 Kevin Leman, *Becoming the Parent God Wants You to Be* (Colorado Springs: NavPress, 1998), p. 107.

8 Quoted in David Clarke, Ph.D., *Winning the Parenting War* (Uhrichsville, OH: Promise Press, 1999), p. 86.

9 Warren Wiersbe, "Be" Series, NT, Volumes 1 & 2 (Colorado Springs: Cook Communications, 1989).

MIDDLE SCHOOL–
A TIME TO LISTEN

$\simR$

Chapter 4

AS JENNIFER MOVED from elementary to middle school, the sound of my daughter's voice became . . . extremely talkative! I can remember many slumber parties and other times when Jennifer's friends gathered in our home. It was nonstop talking, and my daughter's voice was usually the leading tone.

This was okay with us, since we knew that Jennifer's strengths involved being with people and communicating. These years were difficult as Jennifer moved from being a little girl into becoming the independent teenager of middle school.

Welcome to puberty! It's the time when a child's body changes drastically and starts to develop into adult size, shape, and sexual potential. It can begin as early as 9 or 10 years old or as late as 17 or 18. Usually girls reach puberty earlier than boys do. Most children have a "growth spurt" during puberty when they gain weight, then height, and then significant muscle mass. Their legs usually grow first, then the torso. In girls, hips grow wider; in boys, shoulders grow broader. The head grows in length and breadth, the nose and jaw also grow. The first sign in girls is usually the growth of breasts. Internal organs grow, too—the heart and lungs increase in size; sweat glands become more active, especially those in the armpits. The sex organs become much bigger; hair begins to grow in the groin area and armpits. A boy's voice will deepen, and facial hair starts poking through.

Young people have little time to adjust to these rapid physical changes and are sometimes unaware of their size and strength. And coordination may lag behind! You'll notice that Junior is bumping into things a lot (and breaking a few knick-knacks around the house, without meaning to). He'll also need more food to fuel these changes. Such rapid changes in their bodies may embarrass young people. So we parents need to prepare them to expect these changes and be ready to discuss openly any confusing feelings they may have.

This is a time when we as parents need to minimize conflict as much as possible. Teenagers are often upset, confused, frustrated, and depressed as they try to figure out what it means to be an adult and face problems on their own. At this point, they're existing in two worlds at once: sometimes surprising us with their childishness, at other times displaying incredible maturity. It can be difficult to know how to respond to these ups and downs. Arguing, ordering, lecturing, ignoring, or being angry with teenagers won't help. Instead, show them you understand (or are *trying* to understand) by:

Listening to them;
Showing you are listening by looking at them;
Talking about the feeling as well as the action;
Not assuming you know the meaning of what they say—let them tell you;
Not judging or analyzing them;
Asking about their interests and opinions, without prying;
Sharing your own feelings with them;
Asking good questions.

Teenagers should also remember that shouting at and ignoring their parents won't help, either. Since the sound of my daughter's voice was very talkative, we needed to develop some good listening skills.

This is true even if your middle schooler *isn't* a talker. Puberty is such a time of transition for the child that parents need to make a firm commitment to move into a brand new way of relating. No longer will it be possible to keep our communication the familiar one-way street in which we do all the telling, all the ordering, and all the teaching. It's time for communicating on a two-way street, and it all starts with good parental listening.

Hearing . . . But Listening Too?

We spend 70 percent of our time communicating, and of that, we spend almost all the time (70 percent) in listening. However, how well are we really listening? One of my favorite teachers in high school was Miss Hempstead. She was such a fantastic English teacher because of her ability to listen, *really listen*. When we talked with her, she looked us straight in the eye, and it was as if the whole world revolved around us at that moment. While taking in our words, she did more than that: she put her entire being into focusing on who we were at the moment.

Listening to your children this way is critical. When they come to you with a problem, an idea, or just to talk, they need to feel that they have just stepped into the center of your universe. They need to know you're focused on them and nothing else; that you understand. For them not to know, and I mean absolutely know, that they are understood can be terribly frustrating. We live in an area close to the beach, and we often need to drive in the fog. We know the streets and highways well; however, in the fog, our familiar landscapes seem to break apart. We feel disoriented; we fear we'll hit something. And even on familiar turf, we can't "see" where we are going or measure how far we have gone. The same is true for children as they attempt to communicate to a non-listening parent. A dense fog traps them, and they can't see where to go. Life in a constant fog isn't fun, and life with a parent who doesn't really listen isn't fun either. Children need to know that you are listening to them and making every attempt to understand them.

Yes, listening is so important that we need to delve into it much deeper. What does it really mean to listen, and how can we do it better? Let's consider four categories that comprise our task: godly listening, active listening, effective listening, and next-step listening. If we can master these skills, we'll be well on our way to some great communication with our young teen.

Godly Listening

Anyone who is willing to hear should listen and understand!

—Matthew 11:15 (NLT)

Jesus is giving public testimony to John the Baptist here. He ends His testimony by telling the people to "listen up!" They need to be "willing to hear." That means setting aside any preconceived ideas or prejudices. If we're not willing to hear, then everything someone says to us will go right past our ears, and we won't have a clue what he or she is trying to communicate. God gave us two ears and one mouth. Too bad that most of the time we use our mouths twice as much as our ears! Ever recall telling a story and knowing for certain that your listener is spending your precious time forming his own comeback? Such people aren't "willing to hear." Their only interest is in what *they* have to say.

Let it not be so with our teens! No matter how trivial the issue may seem, we need to focus on it—and on the one who's burdened with it. As we demonstrate, over time, our willingness to hear, then when the larger issues come forward our children will trust enough to confide in us. No matter what the sound of our child's voice, we need to be willing to hear.

Secondly, in the passage above Jesus reminds the crowd that they "should listen." Jesus had just delivered a powerful message, stating that He was God's Son and the Savior. Not a trivial message! Yet our children's messages to us, no matter how much less world-changing, should never be trivial in our eyes. Years ago I watched a video presentation by leadership expert Tom Peters. One segment featured a well-respected elementary school principal who obviously loved children. One way he showed respect for what the children had to say was this: he never looked down to them while they were talking. He got down on his knees and looked them right in the eye from their level. What a great way to listen! I am a tall man, and I found that this technique really helped me focus my attention on my children and give them a sense of acceptance.

The last part of the Matthew verse says "understand." This word is often translated from the biblical Greek as "hear," but it should carry with it a bit of an accusatory tone. The word implies a *responsibility* to do the action and perceive what is going on. For example, we can "hear" the wind. In this case, the word would mean not only hearing the wind (the physical act of hearing) but perceiving the wind as well. So Jesus was saying His audience needed to hear *and* understand, and so do parents today. If we don't understand, or take the time to *try* to understand, then the moment of communication, of teaching and of encouragement, is lost.

Jesus speaks of listening two other times in Matthew. In verses 13:9 and 43, He reiterates the importance of hearing, listening, and understanding as He speaks to the crowds. Children have the same expectations of parents. They want their parents' full attention, hearing, and understanding. The Book of Proverbs says:

> *He who gives an answer before he hears,*
> *It is folly and shame to him.*
>
> —Proverbs 18:13 (NASB)

In this text, the word "hear" refers to the physical act of hearing. However, the author of Proverbs gives the reader some consequences for not *listening*. The first is folly. This Hebrew word, *iwwelet,* means foolishness or stupidity. It can mean foolishness in violating God's law, or it can describe the activities and lifestyle of a person who ignores the instructions of wisdom. The parent who answers before she hears (in other words, chooses not to listen) is deciding to ignore the instructions of wisdom.

The second consequence is shame. The derivative translation of this Hebrew word is *kelimma,* meaning "confusion, dishonor, reproach." It can also mean insult. The writer is telling us that if we answer before listening, we won't only feel shame, but also we will insult the person who is talking. What a terrible way to communicate with children! For the parent to feel shame is wrong and for the child to feel insulted is a double whammy to self-esteem, the relationship, and the future of communication.

I always hurt when I hear parents talk about how they can't communicate with their teenagers. Studies show that one of the greatest complaints of teenagers is: "Mom and Dad just don't listen to me!" Therefore, both sides are feeling the pinch. My firm belief is that this happens because the parents didn't take the time to develop good listening skills when the children were small. Instead, the parents may have unwittingly created folly, shame, and insult. The Apostle James adds his own insight into the qualities of good listening. He writes:

> *¹⁹ My dear brothers and sisters, be quick to listen, slow to speak, and slow to get angry.*
> *²⁰ Your anger can never make things right in God's sight.*
> *²¹ So get rid of all the filth and evil in your lives, and humbly accept the message God has planted in your hearts, for it is strong enough to save your souls.*
> —James 1:19-21 (NLT)

• *Be quick to listen.* This is a reminder of what we've previously studied. The original biblical word for "quick" means "speedy." We should be speedy to listen. There's a sense of urgency here. I used to play league softball with a former champion sprinter. He generated a huge burst of speed out of the batter's box and usually beat out infield ground balls, turning easy outs into hits. He was the speediest person I have ever known over a short distance. The Apostle James is encouraging us to a burst of speed when it comes to being ready to listen. Proverbs 17:28 says, "Even a fool is thought wise if he keeps silent, and discerning if he holds his tongue" (NIV).

•*Be slow to speak.* How many of us jump to conclusions before we've heard the full story? We leap to some conclusion before we know all the facts. When I was seventeen, I was a passenger involved in a serious car accident. I can still remember an injured girl's father as he came running into the emergency room asking if I had been driving. He was livid with anger toward me—and I was just a passenger. When he found out the facts (first, that his daughter had limited injuries, and second, that I had not driven) he cooled down. However, he could have made a serious mistake in his quick anger before he listened to all of the facts. Proverbs 13:3 says, "He who guards his lips guards his soul, but he who speaks rashly will come to ruin" (NIV).

• *Be slow to get angry.* James recalls the same word to address our anger. We are to be quick to listen, but slow to speak and slow to get angry. However, he adds some punch to the consequence of anger. He says in the next verse that you don't accomplish anything with God when you are angry. Moreover, I might add, that parents don't accomplish anything with their children when they are angry. All too often, blowups lead to things being said that hurt our children deeply. These outbursts are hard to repair and could be avoided totally if we as parents just set our anger aside. Proverbs 10:19 says, "When words are many, sin is not absent, but he who holds his tongue is wise" (NIV).

• *Save your souls.* Here James then gives the reader a wonderful benefit. We see the promise of strength if we are slow to speak, slow to anger. The Greek word for "save" is also translated "heal." The ability to heal your relationship is right before you if you take the time to listen and be slow to respond. Take the test—listen, don't speak, and don't get angry—just listen and see God's benefit, the benefit of healing and strength. Proverbs 29:20 says, "Do you see a man who speaks in haste? There is more hope for a fool than for him" (NIV).

Many times when our children were allowed to simply talk, they worked out a problem themselves. More often than not, when we just listened, our children thought through what they had done (in the case of poor behavior) or thought through the right solution (when facing problems). We could simply listen, affirm, and encourage them instead of yelling or offering immediate solutions.

Active Listening

Listening does not need to be a passive activity. It can be a rather action-oriented part of the communication process. When we actively listen to others, we try to find out all the details and develop those details into further conversations and more details.

If you take control of the conversation, you'll often miss the objective completely. I can remember times when I came to a conversation with one of my children fully prepared to deliver a "perfect solution." When the discussion finished, however, my child was very unhappy. My attitude had been, "Don't confuse me with the facts, my mind is already made up." I forgot how to listen, and it cost me dearly. In addition, it takes much longer to repair the relationship than it would have if I had listened in the first place. I have found that two skills are necessary for good, active listening—

Skill #1: Asking Questions

Asking questions is a vital sign of curiosity, and we will never be able to learn anything unless we are first curious about it. When our children have been in school all day, are we curious about what happened? Can we ask questions in order to better serve our own curiosity? Questioning, in this sense, is a valuable skill for parents.

Actually, many parents make the mistake of talking too much. They overstate and don't take the time to listen and ask good questions. I have spent most of my career in business, and selling is a major part of any good business. One characteristic that I see in the best sales personnel is the ability to be great listeners and ask excellent, fact-finding questions. Sounds backwards, doesn't it? Sales people are supposed to be great talkers, right? WRONG. Great sales people listen, and they skillfully reveal their customer's needs. They do that by asking good questions and actively listening.

Basically, people love to feel that what they are saying is important. Children want to be encouraged and helped by their parents. By questioning your children, you are letting them know that you are interested in them and their needs. You're not just pushing for information. Rather, you gently begin pulling answers out of them, with no pushing even necessary.

Over the years, I have categorized some questioning techniques. These methods have helped me learn to ask questions, which enables me to keep the conversation rolling and dig for more information. What are these tried and true questioning techniques? There are plenty, but I think you'll benefit from using at least these four in your family interactions:

1. *Tying down the details*. Asking this type of question can tell you whether you fully understand what your child is saying. For example, you may say, "You want to go outside and play for an hour, is that right?" You not only restate something the child has said, you ask a question for clarification of details. When you get agreement, you can be certain that you are both on the same page. If you receive a blank stare or a confident "that isn't what I said," then you know you have some more talking to do. Some of the most effective tie-downs are as follows:

Isn't it?	Doesn't it?	Hasn't he?	Haven't they?
Don't you?	Didn't you?	Shouldn't we?	Couldn't we?
Isn't that right?	Won't you?	Is that it?	Do I have it right?

The goal is to get an agreement between what *he thought* he was saying and what *you thought* he said. You can then follow up a tie-down question with another question, but at the very least, you are showing your child that you are listening, and that both of you are agreeing on what has been said or promised.

2. Offering an alternate choice. In dialogue with your child, an alternate choice allows you to ask a question with two different choices. It helps the child begin to use discernment, and it helps the conversation become much more of a two-way dialogue. This technique, like the previous one, also helps the parent get some details. For example, "You want to play soccer with Jimmy, don't you? Will you want to go Saturday or Friday after school?" Remember the goal is to enlist your child in conversation, to let him or her know you are actively listening instead of fleeing, and to get to some details.

Alternate choice also lets you set some parameters. For example, suppose you know that only a few solutions will solve a problem, but you may not want to dictate a solution. Here the alternate choice question allows you to present a few acceptable solutions as options for the child to choose. It allows you to guide the child while giving over some power.

Alternate questions also get you out of the habit of asking open-ended questions, which could lead you all to areas where you may not want to go, or open the discussion too wide for the reality of the moment. "Where do you want to go for dinner?" opens the discussion much more widely than, "Would Mexican or Chinese be better tonight?" It's amazing how our wording choices can help us avoid arguments. Let's say that your son does not like to read, but he needs to read a book for school. Rather than attacking his lack of interest, find two great books and bring them home saying, "Which one of these would you find most interesting?"

3. *Using easily answered questions.* Your child is a source of loads of information. How will you draw it out?

Using "easily answered questions" is a great facilitator here. It involves employing the old Socratic method of learning and teaching. Using easy questions flushes out information and leads the child to a valuable teaching moment. Using easy questions also keeps the conversation flowing and thus lets the child know how loved and appreciated she really is.

Easily answered questions allow parents to help their children sort through all the messages they're receiving, whether from peers or mass media. Parents can ask some simple, loving questions and help their children make decisions and understand *why* they made the decisions. The bottom line is that if children fail to sort through all they are hearing, feeling, and seeing they may make some wrong choices. This failure to act upon the right information hurts them and their parents. It can ultimately lead to life-changing, damaging choices, all because of failure to ask a few simple questions.

Should parents find it difficult to ask these questions, a good tip is to start with the five "w" questions. Using "Who," "What," "When," "Where," and "Why" questions can be an easy way to start conversations or find out more information.

4. *Asking "IF" questions.* Sometimes it isn't easy to talk to our children. They may require an environment where there is no risk. "If" questions take your children out of reality and ask them to use their imaginations to answer hypothetical questions. "If we were going to let you go to the concert, how would you get there?" is an example of an "If" question. We are probing for their best guess, not the pressure of the right answer, right at this moment. "If" questions allow us to ask our children to imagine what it would be like and respond accordingly. This forms the basis for discussing the issues without so much emotional attachment.

"If" questions help parents open up the communication and test the waters before making needed decisions. They also get parents out of the "telling" mode and into the "asking" mode. And they're easy to build. Simply start with "If" and then lead in to the possible answer. "If you were allowed to go . . .

when would you . . .

how would you . . .

where would you . . .

who would you . . . and so on.

Questions are ways for parents to engage their children. However, what about kids who just won't open up? How can parents get them to talk? Norm Wright and Rex Johnson, in their book, *Communication, Key to Your Teens*, write the following about a character they call Silent Sam:

> *Many [parents] have said, "I would love to communicate, but how can you with a brick wall?" If your teenager fits this description, ask yourself the question, What is his silence saying? What is the message behind the silence? It could communicate love, satisfaction, well-being, pouting, sulking, indifference, hostility, bitterness, or fear.*
>
> *What can you do to help the silent member open up? Saying "Talk to me" usually doesn't help. Ask for opinions and avoid questions that can be responded to with a "yep" or "nope." Ask, "What do you think about. . . ?" or "What would you suggest . . .?" If he says, "I don't know," you could offer three or four suggestions.*
>
> *Don't put pressure on your teenager. You might say, "I am willing to talk with you, so when you feel you would like to talk, let me know." Then back off, pray for an abundance of patience, and wait.[1]*

Skill #2: Seeking First to Understand

I first learned about this concept when I read Steven Covey's best-selling book *Seven Habits of Highly Effective People*. Covey offers this powerful principle, which is best conveyed in his own words:

> *Seek First to Understand, Then to Be Understood is the endowment of courage balanced with consideration. Does it take courage and consideration to not be understood first? Think about it. Think about the problems you face. You tend to think, "You need to understand me, but you don't understand. I understand you, but you don't understand me. So let me tell you my story first, and then you can say what you want." And the other person says, "Okay, I'll try to understand." But the whole time they're "listening," they're preparing their reply. They are just pretending to listen, selective listening. When you show your home movies or tell some chapter of your autobiography—"Let me tell you my experience"—the other person is tuned out unless he feels understood. What happens when you truly listen to another person? The whole relationship is transformed: "Someone started listening to me and they seemed to savor my words. They didn't agree or disagree, they just were listening and I felt as if they were seeing how I saw the world. And in that process, I found myself listening to myself. I started to feel a worth in myself."*
>
> *The root cause of almost all people problems is the basic communication problem—people don't listen with empathy. They listen from within their autobiography.[2]*

Parents need to learn empathetic, active listening with their kids. By putting aside their own desire to be heard, parents can learn from their children as well as develop a strong bond of mutual trust. Children want to be heard, they seek our approval, and they want someone to confide in. When we don't seek first to understand, we put them on the defensive.

Effective Listening

To be a good listener you need to "want" to hear. You can try all you like, but unless you make an active effort to hear, you will never be a good listener. Our new teenagers are beginning to feel some sense of independence. They want to stretch their new muscles and begin the process of moving away (emotionally and physically) from their parents. Listening will be the bridge in the communication process. It will allow us to "hear" what is going on in their lives and become aware if there are areas needing our teaching and help. However, we must listen carefully so we completely understand the needs before jumping in with solutions. Here are some basic listening tips you can start using today:

• *Look at the speaker.* The whole process begins with giving your child undivided attention. Don't check e-mail, phone mail, snail mail, or watch the news while your child is speaking to you. Set aside time to focus completely on Susie and what she's saying. Make eye contact and watch body language. If you don't have time now, be honest with her and schedule a time when you will be able to give her your undivided attention. Then keep your word and don't miss your appointment.

• *Don't interrupt.* According to author and speaker John Maxwell, people interrupt for one of three reasons: (1) they don't place enough value on what the other person has to say; (2) they want to impress others by showing how smart or intuitive they are; (3) they're too excited by the conversation to let the other person finish talking.

We need to examine our motives for interrupting our children. We need to give our children time to express themselves fully and without hurry or interruption. Lastly, as I said before, don't use the speaker's time to develop your own response. Good listening isn't problem solving; it's relating.

- *Focus on understanding.* In general, people don't remember what other people say to them. Studies at several major universities show that people remember only 50 percent of what they have heard, and this drops to 25 percent by the next day. As the Steven Covey quote earlier in this chapter points out, good listening requires us to focus completely on understanding what the speaker (in this case your child) is saying. Any other focus, even on being understood yourself, is a waste of time and won't help the communication process.

- *Determine the need at the moment.* Many times a person will begin talking to you for reasons that aren't immediately apparent. While you are listening, it is a good idea to discover why this person has chosen *this particular moment* for this conversation. Is he venting? Is she hurting? Or, is he simply informing you? Determining the need will help you put whatever is being shared into the proper context.

This happens all the time between my wife and me. When we talk, oftentimes, I try to solve her problems and achieve some kind of resolution. But usually Pam is just sharing an experience or an emotion (perhaps just blowing off steam after a long day). When I don't determine the need, I fall into a terrible trap and disappoint her in my response.

- *Check your emotions.* We saw earlier in this chapter that God doesn't want us to communicate out of anger. It really can get in the way of effective listening and can produce a terrible response. The best thing to do is take a deep breath and check your emotions before your children begin to talk.

- *Suspend your judgment.* You can't jump to conclusions and be a good listener at the same time. This is true if you listen from your own autobiography rather than to what your child is actually trying to tell you. I could always tell when my father was listening from his past rather than from my present. He would give me needless warnings about things that came from his teen years rather than truly listening and learning from me. I understand now that his motives were pure; he was trying to help me avoid some dangerous pitfalls. But his approach wasn't as effective as it could have been, especially with a teenager trying to assert his independence.

• *Sum up at major intervals.* A good technique is to give the speaker some feedback at major intervals. Don't just sit there and nod your head; rather, "read back," or reflect what you think you have heard the person say. This technique gives you an opportunity to verify what has been said and lets the speaker know that you are actively a part of the conversation.

• *Make listening a priority.* Just take time to listen. Set aside times when you can easily sit down and communicate with your children. Make listening something that is important to you, and it will be the bridge to good communication and understanding. We had evening Bible studies with our children, and after reading Scripture or reading a Bible story, we would have some of the best times of communicating ever. We just let the children talk, and they would take us on journey after journey into their lives, giving us great insight into their needs. These times were a real priority to our family.[3]

Take a tip from me, the next time your teenager comes up to you and wants to talk, be a good listener. It will pay significant, long-term, relational dividends.

Next-Step Listening

Sometimes, as we listen, we need to help our teenagers solve problems. After we have fully listened, our teens may approach us and ask for a solution. On the other hand, you may be having behavioral problems with your teen, and instead of arguing or not discussing the issue at all, you want some tools to help you both out of the situation. At this moment, you need to go from listening to problem solving. Problem solving is a process that helps you and your teenager negotiate solutions to a range of problems and conflicts, from messy rooms to dating rules to talking back.

But remember: Nagging isn't a form of problem solving! Good communication never has come from a nagging parent, since it only serves to upset the parents as much as the teens. Instead of nagging, let your children know that you are only going to tell them once; then carry through on your promise. If a teen does not fully complete the responsibility, then privileges must be restricted. All this, of course, needs to be communicated upfront and can cause some interesting (to say the least) times of communication. Needless to say, the listening requirement goes way up as do the emotions on both sides. Sit tight, however, and let your teenager talk to you.

One of the next steps is negotiation. We need to listen carefully and see if any unreasonable expectations are causing our teens real problems. At times, they may find the need to expand their independence, and negotiation is a great tool (again, after active listening) to help the process. Negotiation requires basic ideas and attitudes:

- Show respect. Cooperation only happens when you respect each other. You both have to be willing to listen, ask questions, and share feelings.
- Talk about the underlying problem rather than trying to win, gain control, or prove you are right.
- Take responsibility for your own actions, decisions, and changes.
- Work at making a decision that is good for both of you.

At times negotiation or next-step listening breaks down. If this happens, stop for a while and take some time away from each other. Go and do or think about something different. Once again, listening needs to be a priority. We set a value on the process when we can just walk away for awhile and not let our anger get in the way. Then, when you get together again:

- Avoid saying things that will upset you both;
- Talk again about the rules for negotiation;
- Find a good time and place to talk;
- Talk about present issues rather than old ones;
- Keep the volume and tone of voice reasonable;

- Say what you feel, exactly as you feel, without making more or less of it;
- Listen to each other.

Listening is a great tool to help parents understand and help their children (not just teenagers). It opens up wonderful opportunities for our children to express themselves and for us to learn about their lives. As we continue to listen, our children will be ready to come to us for nurture and guidance. Thus the cycle will move in a positive direction—toward strong relationships.

Notes

1 Norman Wright and Rex Johnson, *Communication, Key to Your Teens* (Eugene, OR: Harvest House Publishers, 1978), pp. 115 116.

2 Stephen R. Covey, *Seven Habits Revisited: Seven Unique Human Endowments* (Salt Lake City: Franklin Covey Co., 1999).

3 The principles on effective listening were developed with the help of John Maxwell's book *Becoming a Person of Influence* (Nashville: Thomas Nelson Publishers, 1997), pp. 92-95.

HIGH SCHOOL–A TIME TO TEACH, Part I

Chapter 5

AS JENNIFER ENTERED HIGH SCHOOL, the sound of her voice was that of singing. Jennifer had worked hard in her music and her high school career started off with a great choir as well as a great music teacher.

The sound of her voice changed, however, as her high school career progressed. The change started within the school itself. For the first eight years of her school career, Jennifer attended a private Christian school. In the middle of the eighth grade, Jennifer sat down with us and asked if she could attend public school instead. Her main concern was: "How can I make it in the world, if I don't know anything about the world?" After many family meetings and significant times of prayer, we decided to make the change to a public high school.

The new school brought many new problems into Jennifer's life. Most significant was the lack of a group of friends. Over the years in Christian school, Jennifer developed a number of close friendships. All her friends stayed in the Christian school, so Jennifer went to the first day of classes alone for the first time in eight years.

Second, Jennifer had never been exposed to the major problems experienced by so many of our public schools. For the first time she was exposed to harsh language and an environment driven by a different cultural attitude. The school had a number of gangs, and one day when Jennifer was in the girl's locker room two girls approached her. They physically hurt her and verbally lashed out at her. The incident definitely scared her. We reported the event to the principal, and he handled it with care; nevertheless, it forever changed Jennifer. Even though we moved out of that school district (due to a job change) the confrontation taught her some real lessons about her faith and about what it means to call upon God for help in times of trouble.

The sound of my daughter's voice really changed when we were called to move again—this time across the country from California to Michigan. Jennifer had just relocated into a wonderful new high school when I was laid off my job and we had to find employment. The best offer came from a large company headquartered in Michigan, so we hit the road and moved to a new town. Since we were all California natives, Michigan's weather provided a "new" environment.

Jennifer was halfway through her junior year when we moved to Michigan. Now at her third high school in three years, she had a most difficult time (even being the family extrovert) making friends, and we had many crying and praying sessions from that time until graduation. I give her lots of credit for staying with it and not completely losing heart.

These two events—moving from private to public school and moving to Michigan—put tremendous pressure on Jennifer as a teenager. We had some tough going, but through it all, Jennifer's faith increased, and she learned how to put it to work. A good friend of mine calls this type of situation "a time of making our faith our own." It was true for Jennifer; she'd observed her parents' faith over the years. Now she actively took it upon herself to wrestle with her problems (and with God!) in order to develop her own brand of faith. At that point, it wasn't her parents' faith, her pastor's faith, or the church's faith. It was hers. Hardship, trials, patience, perseverance, and prayer stamped it and sealed it forever in her heart.

As parents, Pam and I are very proud of Jennifer. During

this time, she could have made many bad choices. Instead, she chose to look to God and seek His direction for her life. She chose to confide in us and ask us for help and support. She also knew herself and continued to focus on her strengths in spite of the criticism of others. I like to think she made these choices because of all the teaching we had done throughout her life. I also believe there were two keys that we taught her so she could respond the way she did. First, we taught her about God, the topic we'll discuss in this chapter. Second, we taught her about herself, a topic we'll discuss in the next chapter.

We had spent many evenings instilling these values as Jennifer grew up, but both concepts really sunk in while she was going through her high school trials. In addition, they continue to help her as a married woman today. These events stretched her faith. However, knowing about God and knowing about herself freed her from anger and depression and helped her make good choices during some difficult years.

Teaching about God

We took every opportunity to teach Jennifer about God, her Heavenly Father. Almost nightly, we had family devotions and we either read a Bible study or Scripture together. These times allowed Pam and me to teach our children about God while providing opportunity to talk and share feelings. We focused on several things, and I want to share here what we found to be the most important lessons for our children. Specifically, when it comes to teaching about God, what exactly should you teach? I suggest you focus on at least seven areas.

Teach the Power of Salvation
First, we wanted our children to know God intimately, knowing the saving power of trusting Christ for forgiveness and redemption. Looking back, I believe Jennifer asked Jesus into her heart many times, just so she knew she had done it! Pam

and Jennifer had studied Noah's Ark a number of times, and Pam had a way of showing Jennifer how God could bring her into His "safety boat" too. After each session, alone in her room, I believe Jennifer asked Jesus into her heart. It didn't matter to us how many times she prayed that prayer of faith; what was important was that Jennifer was actively seeking God, and that her faith was in His Son Jesus.

By the way, if you haven't trusted Christ, this is the time to do it. John 3:16-18 (NIV) says it all:

> *For God so loved the world that he gave his one and only Son, that whoever believes in him shall not perish but have eternal life. For God didn't send his Son into the world to condemn the world, but to save the world through him. Whoever believes in him isn't condemned, but whoever does not believe stands condemned already because he has not believed in the name of God's one and only Son.*

According to Bible teacher J. Vernon McGee:

> *Now, how does God save? God saves by grace. But God so loved the world, that He gave His only begotten Son that whoever (you can write your name in here and I can write mine) believes in Him shouldn't perish, but have everlasting life. Notice that with the word believe is the little preposition "in" which means to believe "in Christ." That is, we trust Him as the One who bore the penalty for our sins. This is a personal thing. We must each believe that He died in our place and in our stead. My friend, you must believe that He died for you.[1]*

Take a moment, if you haven't trusted Christ, to say, "God loves me." Pray thanking God for His Son Jesus and the wonderful new life He has for you as part of His Kingdom forever.

If you *have* already trusted Christ, or even if you just now received Him, it's time to focus on your child's salvation. Here are some tips if your child has not already trusted Christ for his or her salvation:

- Bathe the decision in prayer. Spend time with God and ask Him to give you special, teachable moments. Also, ask Him to prepare your child's heart for the Gospel message.
- Seek the right moment. Use unique moments to show your child the wonders of God. Freely talk about God with your kids. Help them see God everywhere.
- Don't push; pull. Ever try to push a string across a table top? It's much easier to pull the string than it is to push it. The same is true with our kids. It's much easier if you "pull" them with questions and dialogue, than it is to "push" them into submission.
- Be patient. If they are not receptive the first time, don't lose heart. Continue to pray that God would soften their hearts toward His message.

Teach the Wonder of Creation

Help your children thrill to the wonder and power of creation! It should give them a sense of purpose and a sense that they are special and unique. Genesis 1:26-27 (NIV) says:

> *Then God said, "Let us make man in our image, in our likeness, and let them rule over the fish of the sea and the birds of the air, over the livestock, over all the earth, and over all the creatures that move along the ground." So God created man in his own image, in the image of God he created him; male and female he created them.*

In verse 26, with the last stage in the progress of creation now reached, God said, "Let us make man," words that show the peculiar importance of the work to be done. It was the formation of a being who was to be God's representative, clothed with authority as visible head and monarch of the world.

The phrase, "in our image, after our likeness" has a peculiar distinction. The significance here is that it is mentioned twice. In whom does this image of God reside? It resides in a being who is erect, and who has three distinguishing features—body, soul, and spirit. It means we have a personality and—what is especially unique—the ability to make free decisions. Our children are products of God, as well. They are free to make decisions. Colossians 1:16 (NIV) says:

> *For by him all things were created: things in heaven and on earth, visible and invisible, whether thrones or powers or rulers or authorities; all things were created by him and for him.*

God has given us life, and we were created for Him. You and your children are unique creations of God, one of a kind, created for His glory. Teaching your children about creation not only allows you to share with them that they were created in God's image, but it gives you an opportunity to share a purpose and vision—they were created for His glory. They were not an accident; they were created for Him and for His purposes. What are those purposes? We may not know today, but He assures us that He has a purpose and a plan. That is a real confidence builder!

We are not just accidents, but part of a major plan orchestrated by God Himself, for Himself. If you have wondered why a certain tree has a certain kind of leaf, it's because that is the way He wanted it. He made it, and it was made for Him. Our children need to know this as well—our daughter's red hair is certainly special in light of the fact that neither Pam nor I have red hair. He designed it; He created it for His purpose. No matter how much teasing Jennifer received about her hair, she could remember that He wanted it that way. Psalm 139:13-16 (NIV) says:

> *For you created my inmost being; you knit me together in my mother's womb. I praise you because I am fear-*

fully and wonderfully made; your works are wonderful,
I know that full well. My frame was not hidden from you
when I was made in the secret place. When I was woven
together in the depths of the earth, your eyes saw my
unformed body. All the days ordained for me were writ-
ten in your book before one of them came to be.

Your children need to know that they were fearfully and wonderfully made. During the teen years, change is bombarding their bodies. New feelings, new hormones, new dimensions are all bubbling up at an explosive rate. How can they cope? They can make it by knowing that they are fearfully and wonderfully made by a God who loves them for who they are.

Jennifer successfully coped with so much change, and sometimes rough treatment, because she knew the power of creation deep inside. She knew without a doubt that God had made her in His image. She knew deep down that God created her for His purpose. In spite of her changing body, Jennifer knew that she was fearfully and wonderfully made. She knew that she was "skillfully woven" (v. 15) by a God who ordained her days even before she was born. This teaching gave Jennifer tremendous confidence and hope. Kay Arthur writes:

O, Beloved, if you are not happy with yourself, with
your child [or your children with themselves], or with a
loved one, run into the strong tower of the name of your
Elohim (Proverbs 18:10). The why of it all may have
brought darkness. You may not understand how your
situation could ever bring Him glory, but you can trust
in the name of the Lord.[2]

Teach the Efficacy of Prayer

Prayer has always been a vital part of our lives. The ability to communicate directly with our loving Heavenly Father was something we wanted to impress upon our children from the time we could begin teaching them. We've had many tender moments with our children as we've shared prayer times and seen our requests answered. We've also had amazing times of teaching and learning when God has chosen to answer our requests in His own unique ways.

As Jennifer entered her senior year of high school, we spent many hours praying for her to make friends, find a group, and enjoy her final year. Because of our transfer from California to Michigan, Jennifer needed to take several freshman-level classes. This disrupted her social life, as she couldn't spend her class time with kids her own age. We continued to pray, but the year went by without any changes. Jennifer didn't even attend her senior prom (an important thing for a girl who is outgoing and likes parties) or any other school functions that would normally be a key ingredient in a student's senior year.

God chose to answer our prayers differently than we had hoped. However, in so doing, He gave us the opportunity to teach our daughter about His will, patience, and faith. As a result, even through the tears, we saw Jennifer's faith grow stronger. Jennifer was able to see the power of prayer and how it could shape her into the person God wanted her to be. As C.S. Lewis once said, "Prayer doesn't change God, it changes me." We could see the changes in Jennifer, and they helped her move into the next stage of her life.

We must always remember that God, who knows what is best in a way that we don't, will always answer our prayers by saying "yes," "no," or "wait." If He does say "no," He'll usually provide a different answer than we had even imagined. That is, He has something *better* to give than what we've asked for. This was the case when Christ denied Paul healing for his thorn in the flesh (see 2 Corinthians 12:7-9). We need to remember (and teach our children as well) that to say "Your will be done" is the most explicit way of expressing faith in the goodness of what God has planned.

I believe the teenage years are full of opportunities for us to support and encourage our children, especially through praying for or with them. Many parents I know have a tendency to let go of their children during these years. They see that their children have many friends, or are involved in constant activity, and they start to accept the fact that they'll be taking much less time with their teenagers. I think this is a mistake.

Pam and I found that both our teenagers needed to know we were there for them. Both Jennifer and Zachary experienced life-changing events during the high school years and they both have told us how much they appreciated our support, encouragement, and undergirding prayer for them. Praying for our children is an activity that parents can enjoy for years, and it gives the parents a special connection with the teenager.

Our family has a favorite euphemism for our home. We call it our "safe harbor." No matter if we were in California or in Michigan, our home was (and still is) a "safe harbor" into which our children can sail without fear. Many times, the safe harbor has been the port of prayer as we joined our children in prayers for their trials and troubles. The teenage years are not a time to let go; they are a time to come alongside, providing a safety net as all the change and emotion flow.

So . . . it's time to pray for our children! I can't over-stress the importance of this experience of sharing our fears, frustrations, and desires. The writer of the Book of Hebrews reminds us:

Let us therefore draw near with confidence to the throne of grace, that we may receive mercy and may find grace to help in time of need.

—Hebrews 4:16 (NASB)

Both parents and teenagers need to find that special grace in time of need. For the most part, parents are entering midlife and teenagers are soaring toward adulthood. It's a time of change for both sides, and only God's throne of grace can serve as the bridge necessary for communication and that feeling of safe harbor.

Can you see why I emphasize so strongly the importance

of prayer? Just consider its potential role in any family. . . .

• *Praying for our children is a way to bring our will in line with God's plans.* It's an opportunity to set before a loving God all of their fears and needs. In praying, we allow God to help us see His plan for our children too. We want the best for our children, and so does God. Praying daily for our children can help us clearly see His plans as well as where *our* plans for them may be out of line.

• *Praying for our children is a way to demonstrate our trust in God.* The teenage years bring cars, dates, parties, and other major events into the lives of our children. They are away from home much more, and in many cases either they are driving or a friend is driving. What pressure that puts on us as parents! I can clearly remember when we sent Jennifer out for her first solo driving experience. We were in deep prayer, and that praying forced us to trust God for her safety.

• *Praying with our children is far better than complaining at each other!* I don't know anyone who likes complaining and whining. Parents are just as guilty as teenagers are, though, as we tend to nag and complain about their behavior. Teenagers tend to complain about restrictions and lack of understanding. Exodus 17:3-4 (NASB) describes the roaming Israelites:

> *The people thirsted there for water; and they grumbled against Moses and said, "Why, now, have you brought us up from Egypt, to kill us and our children and our livestock with thirst?" So Moses cried out to the LORD, saying, "What shall I do to this people? A little more and they will stone me."*

Again, the people of Israel complained about their problem instead of praying and completely trusting God. They had followed God's leading into the desert but now doubted His ability to take care of them. Often, giving a problem some careful thought, or rearranging our priorities, can solve it. Discussion and good counsel can solve some problems. But only prayer can solve other problems. We should make a determined effort to pray with our teenagers when we feel like complaining at them, because complaining only raises everyone's level of stress. Prayer quiets both our thoughts and emotions and prepares us all to listen and understand.

• *Praying with our children can help restore flawed relationships.* There were times when we went through some strains in our relationship with Jennifer. It just wasn't right and it needed fixing. Judges 16:28-30 (NASB) says:

> *Then Samson called to the LORD and said, "O Lord God, please remember me and please strengthen me just this time, O God, that I may at once be avenged of the Philistines for my two eyes." And Samson grasped the two middle pillars on which the house rested, and braced himself against them, the one with his right hand and the other with his left. And Samson said, "Let me die with the Philistines!" And he bent with all his might so that the house fell on the lords and all the people who were in it. So the dead whom he killed at his death were more than those whom he killed in his life.*

In spite of all Samson had done, God restored him after he confessed and prayed for help. I don't remember the exact incident, but I do remember a time when, during the high school years, I really hurt Jennifer's feelings. I remember going upstairs, opening her door, and seeing Jennifer sitting on her bed in tears. It broke my heart.

After a conversation about the incident we prayed, she forgave me, and we hugged. I don't think her forgiveness would have come so quickly without God's help through our prayers. He can heal flawed relationships.

The power of prayer is an incredible tool for us as parents of teenagers. I challenge you to resist the temptation to let go of your teenager and embrace him or her with prayer. Make time to pray *for* them as well as *with* them. You will see how God is working, and you will provide your teens with the support, encouragement, and safety they need during this tumultuous time.

Teach the Importance of Trust

As Jennifer began to feel the spirit of independence, and as she walked through the series of trials, we needed to help her understand the power of trust in God. We firmly believe that this is the only way she made it emotionally through such a rough high school time. She learned that her trust was not in herself, or her circumstances, but in the Creator, the One who made her special and unique—the One in whom she could rely every moment of every day. Do you know these things about trust?

• *Trust comes from seeking God in everything.* In Colossians 3:1-2 (NASB), Paul writes:

If then you have been raised up with Christ, keep seeking the things above, where Christ is, seated at the right hand of God. Set your mind on the things above, not on the things that are on earth.

Jennifer had trouble when she took her eyes off the Lord. She experienced real growth and reward when she set her mind on the things above. The word used for "mind" in verse 2 can mean "the faculty of perceiving and judging." It can also carry the significance of "something that is like-minded." Teaching trust to our teenagers focuses their eyes in a godly direction and helps intertwine their minds with scriptural truth.

• *Trust comes from substituting God for everything.* Paul writes in Philippians 3:7-11 (NASB),

But whatever things were gain to me, those things I have counted as loss for the sake of Christ. More than that, I count all things to be loss in view of the surpassing value of knowing Christ Jesus my Lord, for whom I have suffered the loss of all things, and count them but rubbish in order that I may gain Christ, and may be found in

Him, not having a righteousness of my own derived from the Law, but that which is through faith in Christ, the righteousness which comes from God on the basis of faith, that I may know Him, and the power of His resurrection and the fellowship of His sufferings, being conformed to His death; in order that I may attain to the resurrection from the dead.

The original Greek word used for "loss" means valuable cargo on ships. Paul is saying that trusting God for everything is better than any lost valuable cargo—all I need is Christ in all things. Jennifer didn't have to perform to please anyone or us—she simply needed to see God and substitute Him in her life for any other thing that in reality was empty by comparison.

• *Trust comes from serving God in everything.* Jennifer soon found that the more she served others, the better things were for her. She put her own needs aside and trusted God to help her be a servant and to give back many of the blessings God had given to her. Paul, writing in 1 Thessalonians 1:9-10 (NASB), says:

For they themselves report about us what kind of a reception we had with you, and how you turned to God from idols to serve a living and true God, and to wait for His Son from heaven, whom He raised from the dead, that is Jesus, who delivers us from the wrath to come.

Jennifer grew in serving others, and she learned patience as she waited for a "deliverance." Later, we would laugh at some of her high school difficulties; however, they taught Jennifer to serve and wait upon the Lord.

When Jennifer transitioned from high school to college, she began working with the youth at our church. Because of the many trials she had encountered in high school, she had the knowledge and experience to help high school students through the rough times in their own lives. She also got the opportunity to know Deron during this time, as he worked with junior high boys. After two years of friendship, their relationship blossomed into engagement and marriage. All this to say, yes, Jennifer experienced some heartbreaking trials during high school. However, she says God's plan unfolded as she chose to use her trials to serve others.

• *Trust comes by seeing God in everything.* Jennifer had to make some decisions. She could fall into temptations or she could see her God in everything and wait. The writer of Hebrews points out:

> *Choosing rather to endure ill-treatment with the people of God, than to enjoy the passing pleasures of sin; considering the reproach of Christ greater riches than the treasures of Egypt; for he [Moses] was looking to the reward. By faith he left Egypt, not fearing the wrath of the king; for he endured, as seeing Him who is unseen. By faith he kept the Passover and the sprinkling of the blood, so that he who destroyed the first-born might not touch them. By faith they passed through the Red Sea as though they were passing through dry land; and the Egyptians, when they attempted it, were drowned. By faith the walls of Jericho fell down, after they had been encircled for seven days. By faith Rahab the harlot did not perish along with those who were disobedient, after she had welcomed the spies in peace.*
> —Hebrews 11:25-31 (NASB)

We all make choices, and in today's world our teenagers are exposed to choices we never had to make. Jennifer succeeded because we had taken the time to teach her to trust and see God in everything.

Jennifer is a person who can be very self-reliant. Her natural bent is to take every responsibility onto her shoulders and work hard to overcome any difficulties. Trust didn't come easily for her. We needed to show her Scripture, pray with her, and encourage her to trust God in all things. The power of trust helped Jennifer over the hump of high school, and it has helped her today as well.

Teach the Goodness of Renewal

God is in the business of change. If we pray and trust, He will begin to renew us; He will make us more like Him. As I've stated many times, the teenage years are times of significant change. Our teenagers are going through tremendous physical and emotional change. They are learning to make major decisions, and they are looking ahead to a time when they'll be living alone. It takes a great God to help them through this process.

The power of renewal isn't only for teenagers. God has told us that we are never finished, so He is constantly renewing us parents as well. So, what is the power of renewal? How are we renewed?

• *We are renewed as we obey God.* Teaching our children to obey us is hard enough, but none of us will see the fruits of renewal without obedience. And it starts with us as parents. We need to walk the talk before we can expect our children to seek renewal through obedience. The Book of 2 Chronicles tells us about Hezekiah. What a terrific role model he was to the people of Israel!

> *And thus Hezekiah did throughout all Judah; and he did what was good, right, and true before the LORD his God. And every work which he began in the service of the house of God in law and in commandment, seeking his God, he did with all his heart and prospered.*
> —2 Chronicles 31:20-21 (NASB)

It is a matter of focus for both parents and children. The reward is the joy of seeing your teenager renewed through obedience to God. The other reward is seeing yourself changed by God for His purposes.

• *We are renewed for having a vision for God's work.* Nehemiah had a vision for God's work.

> *Then I said to them, "You see the bad situation we are in, that Jerusalem is desolate and its gates burned by*

fire. Come, let us rebuild the wall of Jerusalem that we may no longer be a reproach." And I told them how the hand of my God had been favorable to me, and also about the king's words which he had spoken to me. Then they said, "Let us arise and build." So they put their hands to the good work."

—Nehemiah 2:17-18 (NASB)

Chuck Swindoll writes, "In my Bible, I've circled three vitally important words in verse 17: we, us, and we. In order for him to motivate the city planning commission and the potential employees, he had to identify himself with the need. . . . When you cast blame and criticism, you squelch motivation. When you identify the problem, you encourage motivation."[3] Likewise, parents can have a vision for God's work in their children. They, like Nehemiah, can choose the right way to motivate and in so doing teach their children to have the same vision for God's plan in their lives.

Sometimes, this is as simple as pointing them in the right direction about classes or studies. Other times, I would encourage parents to help their high schoolers develop a purpose, vision, and plan. This will take time; however, the reward will be great as we help our teenagers develop life-goals and see the vision for what God wants to accomplish through them.

• *We are renewed by being filled with the Holy Spirit.* "It is the Spirit who gives life; the flesh profits nothing; the words that I have spoken to you are spirit and are life" (John 6:63, NASB). "The Holy Spirit gives spiritual life; without the work of the Holy Spirit, we cannot even see our need for new life (John 14:17). He reveals truth to us, lives within us, and then enables us to respond to that truth."[4] Parents need to teach their children that the Holy Spirit will reveal truth and help them be renewed. It isn't drugs, or clothes, or friends, or even fast cars, but the renewing power of the Holy Spirit that can make lasting, impacting change in our teenagers.

Teach the Blessing of God's Provision

As we uprooted our family from California, one thing became a thorn in our side—we couldn't sell our house. It took us eighteen months, all our savings, and some timely financial help from some dear friends to finally put that chapter of our lives behind us. Through it all, we had a God who met every need and showed our children the power of His provision.

God provides in amazing ways. During this time, we were living a lesson, and Jennifer could see firsthand whether we were truly trusting God for His provision or not. The Book of 1 Kings chronicles the life of Elijah.

> *In a nation that was required by law to care for its prophets, it is ironic that God turned to ravens (unclean birds) and a widow (a foreigner from Jezebel's home territory) to care for Elijah. God has help where we least expect it. He provides for us in ways that go beyond our narrow definitions or expectations. No matter how bitter our trials or how seemingly hopeless our situation, we should look for God's caring touch. We may find his providence in some strange places![5]*

God provides on His timetable. "When I select an appointed time, it is I who judge with equity" (Psalm 75:2, NASB). We certainly seem to struggle with this concept, but it is one that must be shared with our teenagers. Our society is an "instant" society, and gratification is a high priority for today's teenager (adults as well). Taking the time to teach our children the power of God's timing will help them to gain patience and understanding of how God works. His timing only leads us to the best He has available for us.

Psalm 75:2 above can also be translated, "I will seize the moment." It is God who sets the timetable and God who orders the exact time for everything. An old proverb says, "God is never before His time, He never is too late."

Jennifer could see firsthand how we waited for God's provision and His timing. Because we'd exhausted our savings, we weren't able to help Jennifer with her college tuition. At the time, we felt horrible, we prayed, and together we sought God's help. In His time, He gave Jennifer fantastic job opportunities. She graduated from college debt-free and already had a full-time job (before graduation!). We may never fully understand why God brought this into our lives, but we cannot overstate the blessedness of His provision nor His amazing ways of delivering it. What is even better is that Jennifer will never forget His provision either.

The high school years were indeed difficult ones. Changes in Jennifer's life and ours caused us to pull together. They gave us a great opportunity to teach her about God and how He operates in our lives. However, that was not the only teaching we had to do. The next chapter will move us from teaching about God to teaching Jennifer about herself.

Notes

1 J. Vernon McGee, *John, Volume 1* (Pasadena, CA: *Thru the Bible Books,* 1980), p.58.

2 Kay Arthur, *Lord, I Want to Know You* (Old Tappan, NJ: Fleming H. Revell, 1984), p. 22.

3 Charles R. Swindoll, *Hand Me Another Brick* (Nashville: Thomas Nelson Publishers, 1978), p. 63.

4 *The Handbook of Bible Application* (Wheaton, IL: Tyndale House Publishers, Inc., 1992).

5 *Life Application Notes, Life Application Bible* (Wheaton, IL: Tyndale House Publishers, Inc., 1991).

HIGH SCHOOL–A TIME TO TEACH, Part II

༄

Chapter 6

MOST OF THE QUESTIONS I receive from parents are about teenagers. Therefore I felt it essential to add this second chapter dealing with the high school years so we can thoroughly discuss what we did to help our kids through this time in their lives.

Jennifer had some rough days during high school, and we know, looking back, that teaching her about God helped to provide her with the support she needed to get through. We also know it was important for us to spend time teaching Jennifer about herself and others, as well. God made us unique individuals and we can certainly see the differences among us. Some people want to perform in public, others like to be alone, staring endlessly at a computer screen. Some people like to lead and some like to follow. God gave us all a unique set of personality or temperament idiosyncrasies that make for some interesting combinations. As Paul wrote to the Corinthians:

> *14 Now the body is not made up of one part but of many.*
> *15 If the foot should say, "Because I am not a hand, I do not belong to the body," it would not for that reason cease to be part of the body.*
> *16 And if the ear should say, "Because I am not an eye, I don't belong to the body," it would not for that reason cease to be part of the body.*

*¹⁷ If the whole body were an eye, where would the sense
of hearing be? If the whole body were an ear, where
would the sense of smell be?
¹⁸ But in fact God has arranged the parts in the body,
every one of them, just as he wanted them to be.*
— 1 Corinthians 12:14-18 (NIV)

These verses are usually used to describe a church body;
however, I believe they can also be used to describe the family. How boring it would be if we were all "ears"! God arranges
the parts just as He desires and the differences make us unique
and special. Parents need to help their children know about
themselves and how they can learn to build on their strengths.
They need to help them understand other people so they can
appreciate the benefits that come to us because of our differences in roles and temperaments.

During the high school years, teenagers develop new ways
of thinking about life. Their world starts revolving around
friends and peers; they think more about what other people
are doing and saying; they want to fit in. They may change
their dress, speech, and behavior while working out "who they
are." They often criticize what parents say or believe in. This is
why understanding *who they are in Christ* (as well as who
Christ has made them to be) is vitally important. Teenagers can
be helped during this time by:

Being encouraged to feel good about themselves;
Having their confidence built by being with family, friends,
and other adults;
Starting each day positively;
Sharing hugs, kisses, back rubs, a gentle touch on the arm
or other small positive contacts that may be very brief;
Parents and teenagers keeping their sense of humor;
Being listened to and listening in a caring, respectful way;
Having their friends welcome in their home;
Family members taking opportunities to talk and pray
openly.

Some teenagers find it difficult to make friends. Shy children can appear to be unfriendly, so their peers keep away. Some children are loners and are happy on their own. Teenagers are often judgmental and frequently won't tolerate those who are different. Perhaps they don't like the quiet ones, or those not interested in sports (or whatever). Teaching them about themselves is a great way to help them understand temperament differences. God does not make mistakes, so no matter how He has made a person, that is the right way. Nobody should be looked down on as a "loser." Help your teens understand that it doesn't matter whether they are popular. What does matter is how they have learned to view themselves and how well they accept other people's strengths and weaknesses.

Many teenagers also have difficulty with expressing feelings. Hormones cause drastic changes in a young person's body. These chemicals also affect thinking and feeling, and mood swings are common. All of this takes some time getting used to! Teenagers become aware of themselves as sexual beings and can become concerned that they don't measure up to the ideal images seen on television. Information about pregnancy and other sexually related issues constantly bombard them. Having a firm grasp on who they are and how they have been made will help them to better deal with the issues and not put so much pressure on themselves and on their appearance.

Teenagers might feel very excited about becoming adults—starting a career, making big decisions, getting married. Nevertheless, they may also be anxious about their childhood ending. Lots of fun will be coming to an end; responsibility and hard work are kicking in like never before. They'll need to discover how to enjoy these things. Actually, many teenagers want to experiment with the privileges of adulthood. One of the most difficult lessons of this time is learning to enjoy the *benefits* of adulthood while also learning to accept the *responsibilities*.

In the context of teaching teens about themselves, parents

should talk about relationships and about sexual decision-making. Self-esteem can be very fragile here, so parents should try not to:

Overemphasize physical appearance;
Compare your children to others;
Tease them about changes in their bodies.

David Clarke writes:

It is a fact of life that a teenager's self-esteem is dramatically affected by physical appearance. A teen's constant companion is the mirror. A teenager simply cannot walk past a mirror without looking. Studies have been done to prove it. Teens have been offered fabulous prizes—hundreds of dollars, a new car, a day off from school—if they can just walk past a mirror and not look. They can't do it![1]

In all this, parents need to help their teenagers come to terms with who they are and how to handle situations in which their temperament is different from the other person's (even Mom and Dad's). They need to show them their strengths and weaknesses and help them understand that they are fearfully and wonderfully made by a God who loves them and has a unique plan for their lives.

Teach Them about Themselves

God has made us all with different personal styles or temperaments. It was part of His wonderful plan to create humans with different needs, styles, features, and functions. Some of us like details; others seek the Big Picture. Some of us enjoy hosting friends; others would rather sit in a comfortable chair and read good literature. How will you and your teens deal with this? How about . . .

If I don't want what you want, please try not to tell me that my want is wrong.
Or if I believe other than you, at least pause before you correct my view.
Or if my emotion is less than yours, or more, given the same circumstances, try not to ask me to feel more strongly or weakly.
Or yet if I act, or fail to act, in the manner of your design for action, let me be.
I don't, for the moment at least, ask you to understand me. That will come only when you are willing to give up changing me into a copy of you.
I may be your spouse, your parent, your offspring, your friend or your colleague. If you will allow me any of my own wants, or emotions, or beliefs, or actions, then you open yourself, so that some day these ways of mine might not seem so wrong and might finally appear to you as right—for me. To put up with me is the first step to understanding me. Not that you embrace my ways as right for you, but that you are no longer irritated or disappointed with me for my seeming waywardness. And in understanding me you might come to prize my differences from you, and far from seeking to change me, preserve and even nurture those differences.²

The Apostle Paul wrote to the Corinthians about the issue of understanding each other's differences:

⁴ There are different kinds of gifts, but the same Spirit.
⁵ There are different kinds of service, but the same Lord.
⁶ There are different kinds of working, but the same God works all of them in all men.
⁷ Now to each one the manifestation of the Spirit is given for the common good.
⁸ To one there is given through the Spirit the message of wisdom, to another the message of knowledge by means of the same Spirit,

⁹ to another faith by the same Spirit, to another gifts of healing by that one Spirit,
¹⁰ to another miraculous powers, to another prophecy, to another distinguishing between spirits, to another speaking in different kinds of tongues, and to still another the interpretation of tongues.
¹¹ All these are the work of one and the same Spirit, and he gives them to each one, just as he determines.
                                    —1 Corinthians 12:4-11 (NIV)

Going into some detail about these verses will help us to understand the importance of teaching our children to know themselves. Paul lays a solid foundation for us as he talks about spiritual gifts. They are individually handed out in the presence of the Holy Spirit. Their function is to build the body and they are determined by God's plan.

Temperaments are much the same. Each of us has a God-given temperament. The most important thing to remember is that God is in control. Secondly, differences are okay and can be celebrated. Thirdly, it is always good to remember that *a person's weakness is his or her strength taken to its extreme.* According to David Keirsey:

> *The payoff of such work [understanding the tempera-ments] is that you can look at your spouse [or children], for example, as a different person; someone you don't quite understand, but someone that you can, with a sense of puzzlement perhaps, gradually come to appre-ciate. Similarly, you can gain an appreciation of your offspring, parent, superior, colleague and friend.³*

Understanding Ourselves

Before we can truly help our children understand themselves, we must take some time to understand how God made *us.* What is our own basic temperament? How do we react to any given situation?

• *Direct and Indirect Behavior.* One way of understanding our temperament is to look at the level of directness in our behavior. There is a marked difference between direct and indirect behavior. On a scale from direct to indirect, very direct people seek to control circumstances, information, or other people by taking charge. They step right in and take charge of the situation. Indirect people prefer a slower, easier going pace. They are more tactful and will carefully consider the options before acting.

In analyzing yourself (and your children), one important component becomes a matter of where they would fit on a scale of direct and indirect behavior. The following table will give you guidelines for analyzing direct and indirect behavior:

DIRECT	INDIRECT
Approaches risk, decisions, or change quickly and spontaneously	Approaches risk, decisions, or change slowly and cautiously
Frequent contributor to group conversations	Infrequent contributor to group conversations
Frequently uses gestures and voice intonation to emphasize points	Infrequently uses gestures and voice intonation to emphasize points
Often makes emphatic statements, "This is so!", "I'm positive!"	Often makes qualified statements: "According to my sources . . .", "I think so"
Emphasizes points through confident vocal intonation and assertive body language	Emphasizes points through explanation of the content of the message
Questions tend to be rhetorical, to emphasize points or to challenge information	Questions tend to be for clarification, support, or information

DIRECT	INDIRECT
Expresses opinions readily	Reserves expression of opinions
Less patient	More patient and cooperative
Competitive, confronting, controlling	Diplomatic; collaborative
Most likely to maintain position when not in agreement (argues)	When not in agreement, most likely to go along
Intense, assertive	Understated, reserved
Initial eye contact is sustained	Initial eye contact is intermittent
Most likely to introduce self to others at social gathering	At social gatherings, more likely to wait for others to introduce themselves
Firm handshake	Gentle handshake
Tends to break or bend established rules and policies	Tends to follow established rules and policies
More rapid movements	Slow and deliberate movements
Speaks more quickly, more intensely and often more loudly	Slow speech
"Tell oriented"	"Ask oriented"[4]

To best use this table and the one below, rate yourself for each line on a scale of 1 to 5, with 1 being very direct and a 5 being very indirect. For example, if you are very "ask oriented," give yourself a 5 for that line. Complete each line and add up your score. If you are very direct, your score will be 18. If you are very indirect, your score will be 90. Please understand there are no right or wrong answers.. God made us for His glory, and He has made us to be just what we are.

• *Open and Self-Contained Behavior.* Two other factors need to enter parents' thinking as they seek to understand themselves and their children's temperaments. It is the difference between open and self-contained behavior.

OPEN	SELF-CONTAINED
Self-disclosing	Guarded
Shows and shares feelings freely	Keeps feelings private, shares only on a "need to know" basis
Makes most decisions based upon feelings (subjective)	Makes most decisions based upon evidence (objective)
Conversation includes digressions; strays from subject	Focuses conversation on issues and tasks; stays on subject
More relaxed and warm	More formal and proper
Goes with the flow	Goes with the agenda
Opinion-oriented	Fact-oriented
Easy to get to know in business or unfamiliar circumstances	Takes time to get to know in business or unfamiliar social situations
Approaches risk, decisions, or change slowly or cautiously	Primarily task-oriented
Flexible about how their time is used	Disciplined about how time is used by others
Feels cramped by schedules	Prefers following an established schedule
Flexible expectations about people and situations	Fixed expectations about people and situations
Prefers to work with others	Prefers to work independently
Initiates or accepts physical contact	Avoids or minimizes physical contact
Shares or enjoys listening to personal feelings, especially if positive	Tells or enjoys listening to goal-related stories
Animated facial expressions during conversations	More likely to be expressionless during conversation
Shows more enthusiasm than the average person	Shows less enthusiasm than the average person

OPEN	SELF-CONTAINED
Friendly handshake	Formal handshake
More likely to give nonverbal feedback	Less likely to give nonverbal feedback
Responsive to dreams, visions, and concepts	Responsive to realities/actual experiences/facts
Wants to have fun	Wants power
Likes small talk	Not interested in small talk[5]

Once again, remembering that there are no right or wrong answers, score yourself on a scale of 1 to 5, with 1 being high "open" and 5 being high "self-contained." Once you're done scoring each sheet, you can then look at the following grid and determine what your temperament (or your child's temperament) may be.

```
                    (RELATIONSHIP-ORIENTED)
                           OPEN
                             |
The Relater                  |    The Socializer
  We're all in this together |      Let me tell you what
  so let's work as a team.   |      happened to me.
                             |
INDIRECT ————————————————————————————————— DIRECT
(SLOW PACE)                  |             (FAST PACE)
                             |
The Thinker                  |    The Director
  Can you provide            |      I want it done right and
  documentation              |      I want it now.
  for your claims?           |
                             |
                    SELF-CONTAINED
                    (TASK-ORIENTED)[6]
```

115

When you combine your degree of directness with your degree of openness, a definition of temperament begins to emerge. The grid on page 115 shows four quadrants that represent the four basic behavioral or temperament styles. For example, if you are very open and very direct, you are in the Socializer square. Alternatively, if you are very self-contained and very indirect, then you would be in the Thinker quadrant. Combinations of openness and directness then create the four patterns or temperaments:

- Relater, Amiable, Phlegmatic (Cooperative, supportive, diplomatic, patient, loyal)
- Socializer, Expressive, Sanguine (Outgoing, enthusiastic, persuasive, fun-loving, spontaneous)
- Director, Driver, Choleric (Independent, candid, decisive, pragmatic, efficient)
- Thinker, Analytical, Melancholy (Logical, thorough, serious, systematic, prudent)

Let's take the study a little deeper. Once we know our temperament, it is a good idea to then understand each temperament's strengths and weaknesses.

DIRECTOR—STRENGTHS

EMOTIONS	AT WORK
Born leader	Goal oriented
Dynamic and active	Sees the whole picture
Compulsive need for change	Organizes well
Must correct wrongs	Seeks practical solutions
Strong willed and decisive	Moves quickly to action
Unemotional	Delegates work
Not easily discouraged	Insists on production
Independent and self-sufficient	Makes the goal
Exudes confidence	Stimulates activity
Can run anything	Thrives on opposition
AS A PARENT	**AS A FRIEND**
Exerts sound leadership	Has little need for friends
Establishes goals	Will work for any group activity
Motivates family to action	Will lead and organize
Knows the right answer	Is usually right
Organizes household	Excels in emergencies[7]

RELATER—STRENGTHS

EMOTIONS	AT WORK
Low-key personality	Competent and steady
Easygoing and relaxed	Peaceful and agreeable
Calm, cool, and collected	Has administrative ability
Patient, well balanced	Mediates problems
Consistent life	Avoids conflicts
Quiet but witty	Good under pressure
Sympathetic and quiet	Finds the easy way
Keeps emotions hidden	**AS A FRIEND**
AS A PARENT	Easy to get along with
Makes a good parent (nurturing)	Pleasant and enjoyable
Takes time for the children	Inoffensive
Is not in a hurry	Good listener
Can take the good with the bad	Dry sense of humor
Doesn't get easily upset	Enjoys watching people
	Has many friends
	Has compassion and concern[7]

SOCIALIZER—STRENGTHS

EMOTIONS	AT WORK
Appealing personality	Volunteers for jobs
Talkative, storyteller	Thinks up new activities
Life of the party	Looks great on the surface
Good sense of humor	Imaginative and colorful
Memory for color	Has energy and enthusiasm
Physically holds on to listener	Starts in a flashy way
Emotional and demonstrative	Inspires others to join
Cheerful and bubbling over	Charms others to work
Curious	**AS A FRIEND**
Good on stage	Makes friends easily
Wide-eyed and innocent	Loves people
Lives in the present	Thrives on compliments
Changeable disposition	Seems exciting
Sincere at heart	Envied by others
Always a child	Doesn't hold grudges
AS A PARENT	Apologizes quickly
Makes home fun	Prevents dull moments
Is liked by children's friends	Likes spontaneous activities[7]
Turns disaster into humor	
Is the circus master	

THINKER—STRENGTHS

EMOTIONS	AT WORK
Deep and thoughtful	Schedule oriented
Analytical	Perfectionist, high standards
Serious and purposeful	Detail conscious
Genius prone	Persistent and thorough
Talented and creative	Orderly and organized
Artistic or musical	Neat and tidy
Philosophical and poetic	Economical
Appreciative of beauty	Sees the problems
Sensitive to others	Finds creative solutions
Self-sacrificing	Needs to finish what is started
Conscientious	Likes charts, graphs, figures, and lists
Idealistic	
AS A PARENT	**AS A FRIEND**
	Makes friends cautiously
Sets high standards	Content to stay in the background
Wants everything done right	
Keeps home in good order	Avoids causing attention
Picks up after children	Faithful and devoted
Sacrifices own will for others	Will listen to complaints
Encourages scholarship and talent	Can solve others' problems
	Deep concern for other people
	Seeks ideal mate
	Moved to tears with compassion[7]

These strength tables on pages 117-120 will help you see your strengths and how they fit with each temperament. Strengths are what we want to build upon and use to help others. These tables will also help us to see our children's strengths and appreciate how they are uniquely made.

A note on weaknesses: All temperaments have their share of weaknesses. My personal definition of a weakness is a strength taken to its extreme. On page 122 I have outlined some of the basic temperament weaknesses; however, it is best if we remember the definition of weaknesses. If I am a Director, and my strength is decision making, then my weakness is that strength taken to its extreme—I make too many decisions too quickly. If I am a Thinker, and I am heavily into the details, my weaknesses comes in failing to look at the bigger picture—I see everything in the context of the small details instead of looking at the broader perspective.

God created us with both strengths and weaknesses. He gave us strengths to build upon and weaknesses to help us understand that we need His help. Weaknesses can be overcome. Look at the Apostle Peter. Peter was a Socializer, and he was quick to speak (most of the time he spoke before he thought about it). However, read Peter's epistles. They don't show us a person who doesn't think things through. Instead we find a person who realized his weaknesses, turned them over to God, and allowed Him to develop them into what He wanted them to be. Proverbs 13:18 says, "He who ignores discipline comes to poverty and shame, but whoever heeds correction is honored" (NIV).

TEMPERAMENT WEAKNESSES

TEMPERAMENT	AREAS OF DEVELOPMENT
Socializer	• No follow through • Doesn't see her faults • Talks too much • Self-centered • Poor memory • Fickle and "fair weather" friend • Interrupts and answers for others • Disorganized and immature
Thinker	• Believes he is one of a kind • Easily depressed • Low self-image • Procrastinates • Places unrealistic demands on others
Director	• Needs to tone down • Nothing is his fault • Compulsive worker • Needs to be in control • Doesn't handle people well • "Right" but unpopular
Relater	• Low-key • Not excitable • Resists change • Appears to be lazy • Quiet will of iron • Appears wishy-washy[8]

Once we understand areas in personalities that need maturing and development, we can then help ourselves and our children to bolster their weaknesses. We can also easily see that everyone has areas of development, even you Directors!

"Accept him whose faith is weak, without passing judgment on disputable matters" (Rom. 14:1, NIV). We are called to encourage others by our strengths and be encouraged by their strengths where we are weak. In areas of strength, we should work to build and help others. In the areas of our weakness, we can look for people who have strength in those areas and allow them to help us. As we work with our children who have different temperaments than we do, we should come along- side of them and allow our strengths to reinforce their weaknesses. (By the way, it is really fun to have someone's strength reinforce our weakness. This also raises the other person's confidence, since he or she is working in an area of strength.)

Jennifer's temperament strength is joy. Many times when we were going through trials, Jennifer's joyful countenance would bring our thoughts and emotions to a happier level. She was using her strength to serve our family needs.

Understanding Your Children

Once you get a firm grip on your own temperament, you can then move to teaching your children about their temperaments and what those temperaments mean to them. Once Jennifer understood that she was a Director/Socializer and that details were not important to her, she could then understand why she had to focus on details in order to succeed. This was especially true in her relationship with Pam (a Thinker temperament). When the two of them worked together, Jennifer had to be sure she got the details right or Pam would be frustrated. Pam, on the other hand, needed to make sure she was enjoying the bigger picture along with appreciating the whole process of interacting together. So, each of them developed a level of good expectations about each other by knowing their respective temperaments.

At one point in his ministry, Paul had trouble understanding John Mark—

Barnabas wanted to take John, also called Mark, with them, but Paul did not think it wise to take him, because he had deserted them in Pamphylia and hadn't continued with them in the work. They had such a sharp disagreement that they parted company. Barnabas took Mark and sailed for Cyprus, but Paul chose Silas and left, commended by the brothers to the grace of the Lord. He went through Syria and Cilicia, strengthening the churches.

—Acts 15:37-41 (NIV)

In an earlier time, John Mark had left Paul and Barnabas (Acts 13:13). There are many reasons why he had left the men (some believe he was upset that Barnabas his cousin was not the leader; some say he may have been sick; and others write that the rigors of the trip may have been too much for him). Whatever the reason, Paul was upset and didn't want him to continue with him.

One has to wonder: If Paul had understood John Mark's temperament, would there have been a difference in his attitude? Obviously, Barnabas was a Relater. He was an encourager and a healer. Paul, the Director, had to keep moving; he had to reach whatever goal was in front of him. John Mark appears to be a Thinker or Relater and perhaps felt some strain in having Paul the Director as the leader of the pack.

This is an example of how we must understand our children before we commit ourselves to a course of action with them. If our temperaments are so different, like Paul and John Mark, or Jennifer and Pam, then clashes are inevitable. As parents, we need to fully understand our children's temperaments, so that in the natural course of daily living we don't make mistakes based solely on temperament differences.

Understanding Your Child's Reactions

How will your teen react in certain circumstances? Can you make a prediction based on temperament? Yes! The following table will help us better understand each of the four basic temperaments and how each tends to respond or react.

	Relater	Thinker	Director	Socializer
Behavior Pattern	Open/Indirect	Self-contained/ Indirect	Self-contained/ Direct	Open/Direct
Appearance	Casual Conforming	Formal Conservative	Businesslike Functional	Fashionable Stylish
Space	Personal Relaxed Friendly Informal	Structured Organized Functional Formal	Busy Formal Efficient Structured	Stimulating Personal Cluttered Friendly
Pace	Slow/Easy	Slow/Systematic	Fast/Decisive	Fast/Spontaneous
Priority	Maintaining relationships	The task: the process	The task: the results	Interacting in relationships
Fears	Confrontation	Embarrassment	Loss of Control	Loss of Prestige
Under Tension Will	Submit/Acquiesce	Withdraw/Avoid	Dictate/Assert	Attack/Be Sarcastic
Seeks	Attention	Accuracy	Productivity	Recognition
Needs to Know	How it will affect his personal circumstances	How it works	What is does, by when, what it costs	How it enhances his status, who else uses it
Gains Security by	Close relationships	Preparation	Control	Flexibility
Wants to Maintain	Relationships	Credibility	Success	Status
Support His/Her	Feelings	Thoughts	Goals	Ideas
Achieves Acceptance by	Conformity Loyalty	Correctness Thoroughness	Leadership Competition	Playfulness Entertaining
Likes you to be	Pleasant	Precise	To the point	Stimulating
Wants to be	Liked	Correct	In charge	Admired
Irritated by	Insensitivity Impatience	Surprises Unpredictability	Inefficiency Indecision	Inflexibility Routine
Measures personal worth by	Compatibility with others Depth of relationships	Precision Accuracy Activity	Results Track Record Measurable progress	Acknowledgment Recognition Applause
Decisions are	Considered	Deliberate	Definite	Spontaneous[9]

You can use the chart on page 125 to understand your children's reactions under various circumstances. For example, if you notice your child is generally slow getting ready for school, if the child has a very casual appearance and has a very pleasant demeanor, chances are he is a Relater. If the child is slow but very systematic, dresses conservatively, and wants everything precise, she is a Thinker.

A child's behavioral tendencies should tell you how to relate to your child. A child's behavior isn't always the same, but the behavior you see at any given time will tell you how you can adjust your response and meet the needs of your child.

If your child has a Director temperament, and you need to communicate with him or her, the first thing you want to do is quickly get to the point. In our family, we call it "the bottom line." Many times, as Jennifer was growing up, we had to get to the bottom line with her. We had to get to the high points, have some facts (but not walk through every step), and give her some options. We had to put the decision into her hands, we had to help her save time, and we had to move quickly. Lectures never worked. She just didn't have the time or patience for them. Further, she didn't need details—just the facts and some options so she could make a decision.

As Zachary was growing up, we had to be prepared to walk him through every step. He needs precise information, and we had to be accurate or he wouldn't accept what we were saying. Zachary is a very capable young man, but just having options wouldn't work with him. He needed more guidance in making decisions. He is a Thinker, and he enjoys weighing the facts and studying the points of view.

Learning What Can Cause Tension

Not only do we need to know (and therefore teach our children) how to read and understand reactions, we also need to learn to appreciate behaviors that can cause uptightness in others. The chart below is here to help parents see how their temperaments can affect their child and cause tension. Use the table with a teenager to help him/her understand his/her temperament to see how it might "rub some people the wrong way."

If you are a Director . . .

- To Other Directors—Your tendency to over-control a situation. This may reduce their freedom and ability to control.
- To Socializers—Your concern for results, accompanied by an apparent lack of concern for a motivational or fun environment.
- To Relaters—Your tendency not to take enough time to listen. Your priority of time over relationships.
- To Thinkers—Your being so quick, but perhaps not thorough enough.

If you are a Socializer . . .

- To Other Socializers—Your desire for visibility, especially if it reduces their visibility.
- To Directors—Your apparent lack of results orientation/too emotional.
- To Relaters—Your lack of depth in some of your relationships and your quickness.
- To Thinkers—Your lack of attention to detail; your impulsive tendencies.

If you are a Relater . . .

- To Other Relaters—Your lack of initiative, especially if it means they have to initiate.
- To Directors—Your time engaged in too much small talk.
- To Socializers—Your apparent lack of quickness.
- To Thinkers—Your people/small talk orientation instead of the task.

If you are a Thinker . . .

- To Other Thinkers—Your desire to be more right/correct than they are.
- To Directors—Your slower and more methodical pace.
- To Socializers—Your persistent attention to detail(s).
- To Relaters—Your lack of letting them know how you "feel."

Learning How to Get Along with Others

The next chart will help you not only learn what can irritate your children, but it allows you to evaluate your children and how they can, again, learn to get along with others. This is an important step as we teach our children to know other people. When Jennifer was suffering in high school, the understanding of temperaments helped her to know about other people. It helped her retain her feeling of personal worth (to know who she was in Christ and how God had made her) during some very trying circumstances. You can also help your teenagers gain self-confidence as well as understand others' reactions and needs. As they learn this valuable lesson, they can see how they fit as they also determine areas of their lives that need prayer support.

Socializers	Thinkers	Relaters	Directors
Recognize their difficulty in accomplishing tasks.	Know that they are very sensitive and get hurt easily.	Realize they need direct motivation.	Recognize they are born leaders.
Realize they like variety and flexibility.	Realize they are programmed with a pessimistic attitude.	Help them to set goals and make rewards.	Insist on two-way communication.
Keep them from accepting more than they can do.	Help them deal with depression.	Don't expect enthusiasm.	Know that they don't mean to hurt.
Don't expect them to remember appointments or be on time.	Compliment them sincerely and lovingly.	Force them to make decisions.	Try to divide areas of responsibility.
Praise them for everything.	Accept that they like it quiet sometimes.	Don't heap all the blame on them.	Realize they aren't compassionate.[10]
Remember they are circumstantial people.	Try to keep a reasonable schedule.	Encourage them to accept responsibilities.	
Bring them presents; they like new toys.	Help them not to be the family's slave.		
Realize they mean well.			

There is another way to improve relationships and help our children through the teaching of the temperaments. Each of us has a backup style or temperament that shows itself when we are under pressure. It usually happens when we are the most stressful or out of control. When God confronted

Moses and told him to lead his people out of captivity, Moses' backup style kicked in, and he gave all kinds of excuses why he couldn't do God's bidding. Moses wasn't being lazy or lacking confidence. He was a Thinker, and as he processed the details that God was giving him, he just couldn't understand intellectually why God had given him this assignment. Had Moses been a Socializer, he would have jumped at the opportunity (and perhaps not been as prepared as he had to be). Moses was a Thinker, and his backup style held him in check.

Each temperament has its own primary backup:

Director	Autocratic
Socializer	Attacking
Thinker	Avoiding
Relater	Acquiescing

If a child is a Director, she'll become pushy and dictatorial in her backup style. Her voice becomes level and intense. She is unyielding in her opinions. She focuses on the task and work. So, when you push the Director it can get real ugly, real fast. If you are a Relater, the Director child will rule the house. If you are a Director, look out, because the two of you will have some powerful battles!

Socializers become angry and verbal in backup mode. They employ strong language and gestures, and the volume of their voices greatly increases. If you are a Relater or a Thinker, the Socializer child will come on strong and you will want to run away from the fight. As a parent, you will need to decide when it is practical to hold your ground. If you are a Socializer, both of you will become pretty loud.

Thinkers (like Moses) become avoiders when they're backed into an uncomfortable situation. They'll likely get up and leave the argument rather than stay and fight. Parents who are Socializers or Directors, take note. If your child leaves the room during a disagreement, it may not be a sign of intentional disrespect; he or she may be a Thinker and want to avoid the confrontation.

Relaters will just give in as a backup. They offer compliance rather than cooperation. The classical passive/aggressive behavior could emerge in their backup mode. They will do it, but not the way you want it done, or in a timely manner. Parents who have Relater children should be aware that giving in may not always be a good thing. Make sure your child isn't just giving in because it is his or her backup style.

If you are a Director	If you are a Thinker	If you are a Socializer	If you are a Relater
Learn to listen, be patient	Develop focus on the right things, not just doing things right	Be less impulsive	Be less sensitive to what people think
Develop greater concern for people	Try to respond more quickly	Be more results oriented	Be more concerned with the task
Be more flexible with people	Trust your intuition	Control actions, be less demonstrative	Face confrontation
Be more supportive	Be less fact oriented	Focus attention on details and facts	Be more decisive
Explain "why"	Look ahead	Listen, don't talk so much	Increase pace
Be warmer . . . more open	Be more open and flexible	Slow down pace	Initiate and learn to say "no"

Taking Some Practical Action Steps

In the chart above are steps you can take to help your children overcome some of their temperamental weaknesses. Remember: our definition of weakness is *any strength taken to its extreme.* Below are some ways to take action, communicate, and coach.

All this is meant to increase your family compatibility as well as help your children understand who they are and how specially God made them. By identifying your temperament, you can control how you respond. By identifying your child's temperament, you can see how God made her and trust Him to help you build relationships with her. Once you identify your own temperament, then move ahead to teach your children their temperaments. Remember:

- Know your own temperament and how it relates to your children's temperaments.
- Teach the temperaments to your children and help them fully understand that God made them the way He wanted them to be. No temperament is perfect; God can use them all to His glory.
- Help your children know that they are special and unique. Don't put them in a box.
- Pray with your children about their (and your) weaknesses. Seek God's guidance and help to strengthen each other.
- Seek versatility, the ability to adjust your behavior in order to reduce tensions and meet the needs of your family members.
- Tell your children how much you appreciate their temperament. There are areas in which they can excel, and you need to reinforce positive behavior in those areas.
- Find opportunities to put children in their areas of strength.

The end benefit is being available to meet needs. Once you learn how to respond and how your child will respond (normally or under pressure) you can then be available to meet needs. Teaching your child about the temperaments will help them know how to respond to others as they gain a clearer picture of themselves. Finally, I encourage you to take to heart these fine words from James Dobson:

Much has been written about the search for identity, but I doubt if your ten-year-old has read much of that literature. Consequently, you will need to talk about what it means to know yourself. The child with a good sense of identity is acquainted with personal goals, strengths, weaknesses, desires, hopes and dreams. He could sit down and write a paper entitled, "Who am I?" without bogging down in the first paragraph. A child who has been given a meaningful self-awareness by parents and teachers knows where he's going and how he expects to get there. This is a fortunate individual in this day of gray, indistinct self-awareness. . . . It is your job as a parent to provide your child with a healthy identity during the formative years in the home.[11]

Notes

1 David Clark, *Winning the Parenting War* (Uhrichsville, OH: Promise Press, 1999), p. 194.

2 Excerpted from David Keirsey, *Please Understand Me, II,* 1998.

3 Ibid.

4 Jim Cathcart, *Relationship Selling, How to Get and Keep Customers* (Costa Mesa, CA: HDL Publishing, 1988), p. 22.

5 Ibid.

6 Ibid, p. 26.

7 Tables on temperament strengths from Florence Littauer, *Personality Plus* (Grand Rapids, MI: Fleming H. Revell, 1999), pp. 24-27.

8 The charts on weaknesses are from Florence Littauer, *Personality Plus,* pp. 86-140.

9 Jim Cathcart, *Relationship Selling,* p. 27.

10 This table is a compilation of ideas from several sources: *Personality Plus!* by Florence Littauer; *Social Style/Management Style* by Robert and Dorothy Grover Boulton; *Relationship Selling,* by Jim Cathcart.

11 James Dobson, *The New Hide or Seek* (Grand Rapids, MI: Fleming H. Revell, 1999), pp. 176-177.

COLLEGE–
A TIME TO COACH

Chapter 7

WHEN JENNIFER WENT OFF TO COLLEGE, she carried with her a secure knowledge of who God was and a deep love of her Lord Jesus Christ. She also knew who she was and had a grasp of her strengths and weaknesses. Because of this, she was ready to go to the next level.

It was time, once again, for our relationship to change. Jennifer didn't need a parent/child relationship; she needed us to develop a relationship in which she was free to make decisions and yet free also to seek our advice and counsel. She needed a *coach*. She needed us to be her mentors, and she needed to feel that she was empowered, by us, to move out into her newfound independence. Jennifer also needed someone to help her navigate the waters ahead—both in terms of understanding where she wanted to go, and help understanding how to set a vision.

Marian Wright Edelman, arguably the nation's leading advocate for children, believes in the importance of being your child's mentor. She writes:

> *My parents were like the oak tree that the theologian Howard Thurman once described. Its leaves died each fall but stayed on the branches all winter, through wind and snow. It was the business of that tree to hold on to those leaves—not turning them loose until spring, when new buds would unfold.*

Like that tree, my parents hung onto their children until we could blossom on our own. When I think of them, I think of integrity, consistency, common sense, high expectations, study, service and play, sacrifice and bedrock faith. [1]

Isn't that the way to be remembered? We're talking about a unique balance between over-parenting and letting go; however, Ms. Edelman's story of the oak tree helps us to realize that God's timing is the best timing. We parents need to be discerning and ready to move into this role of coaching our children as they begin moving into young adulthood. We cannot completely let go until they are ready to blossom.

Proverbs 15:22 (NASB) says, "Without consultation [coaching], plans are frustrated, but with many counselors [coaches] they succeed." We wanted to step into this role and found that coaching actually encompassed three roles: the role of the mentor, the role of the empowerer, and the role of the navigator. Each role met specific needs for Jennifer as she went through these years. Each role had a purpose, and each role enabled us to help Jennifer blossom and bear significant fruit in her life.

The Role of the Mentor

As Jennifer moved from high school to college, I could see some real changes in her. She was stepping into the final phase of her educational career. Since we had taught her about temperaments, we were sure of some of the directions she'd likely choose, but an entire field of possibilities lay ahead of her. Later, she would make decisions on moving out of the house and also make career plans. Lastly, new emotional needs surfaced during these years.

All this meant that our role needed to change as well. It's quite different having a twenty-year-old in the house as compared to a pre-puberty child. We had to make adjustments in how we treated Jennifer. We were compelled to move into mentoring.

We will look at four components of the mentoring task: vision, determination, priorities, and accountability. I believe these four concepts helped us to mentor Jennifer through the college years and, building on her already solid foundation, gave her the character qualities to live a Christ-centered life despite the world's pressure to do otherwise.

Vision — Seeing Things Clearly

We needed, as mentors, to show Jennifer two aspects of vision. First, we needed to help her see beyond the majority and be comfortable with the minority role. Here's what I mean: she's a Christian, and her faith would be tested as never before. We needed to reinforce all the nights of Bible study and devotional readings. Jennifer would encounter a culture in college that was based upon a thoroughly post-Christian worldview, and we needed to help her maintain a strong commitment to her faith.

Secondly, we needed to mentor Jennifer's vision for the future. Yes, there are college counselors, but we wanted to be active in the process as well. We didn't want to make the decisions; we simply wanted Jennifer to feel comfortable using us as consultants for her decision-making, so she'd *have the means to make good decisions*. We also wanted our mentoring to help her expand her vision beyond the things that were in the present.

In the Bible we can learn about these things from the life of Joseph the carpenter, a great man who could see beyond the majority opinion.

> *Upon learning of Mary's pregnancy, Joseph, being a righteous man, sought to put her away without public disgrace. His response to God's assurances in a dream further demonstrated his piety and character (Matthew 1:18-25).*

135

Joseph took Mary to his ancestral home, Bethlehem; was with her at Jesus' birth; and shared in the naming, circumcision, and dedication of the child (Luke 2:8-33). Directed through dreams, Joseph took his family to Egypt until it was safe to return to Nazareth (Matthew 2:13-23).

As dedicated father, he was anxious with Mary at the disappearance of Jesus (Luke 2:41-48).

Joseph does not appear later in the Gospels, and it is likely that he died prior to Jesus' public ministry."[2]

Joseph surely faced criticism and ridicule from the community around him. Remember that there are three stages to an orthodox Jewish wedding. There is the engagement period, the betrothal, and finally the marriage. The betrothal period can last up to a year, and it is a time to secure the pledge of the engagement. Any woman found pregnant during this time would be suspect to gossip and ridicule. As Joseph thought about it, he mulled over in his mind the possibility of a "quiet" divorce.

But then Joseph had a vision, and his vision gave him the ability to see clearly, beyond the majority opinion. Five things made Joseph a man of vision (1) his relationship with God (see Matthew 1:19a); (2) his respectful attitude toward Mary (see Matthew 1:19b); (3) his sensitivity to God's direction (see Matthew 1:20-23); (4) his obedience to God's will (see Matthew 1:24); and (5) his desire to glorify God (see Matthew 1:25). Joseph was a man with vision, and the majority opinion didn't impair his vision. The only opinion that mattered to Joseph was God's opinion.

It's important for parents to help their children have clear vision from a Kingdom perspective. Especially as they enter the college years, their faith will be tested. Circumstances in both high school and college tested Jennifer's faith. She took one class, for instance, in which a professor took a sexuality poll. The class hadn't a thing to do with sexual behavior, so the professor was simply prying into the private business of his students for no apparent good reason. Jennifer refused to take the poll and reported the incident to her counselor. Unfortunately, the counselor couldn't see Jennifer's embarrassment nor could he share in her high character. However, Jennifer remained strong in the face of criticism and peer pressure. Just like Joseph, Jennifer had the right vision. She chose to go against the majority while remaining sensitive to God's priorities.

Determination — Hanging Tough, Regardless

As vision is being taught, so must determination be modeled and encouraged. "Determination" means to keep on seeking without compromising or taking your eye off your God-given vision and His will. "When the objective is good and the motive is pure, there isn't anything more valuable in the pathway leading to genuine success than persistence and determination." [3]

Yes, it would often be easier just to quit. We hit obstacles and we lose interest. Or we're criticized for what we're doing and we just let the crowd dictate our dreams instead of staying the course and completing it—hanging tough.

When I was in the eighth grade, we had to take mandatory physical fitness tests. We had to do sit-ups, pull-ups, run, jump, and perform other agility checks. My friends and I were all in great shape and very athletically inclined. We easily made all the sports teams and weren't worried about these tests.

A new boy joined our gym class about the time of the first test. Ted (not his real name) wore a cap all the time, not because of fashion, but because he had no hair. Ted walked clumsily and sometimes needed a cane because he suffered from a brain disease. When it came time for the tests, my friends and I made great scores and were proud of our accomplishments. Ted struggled through the tests and scored poorly.

But when it was time to receive our first quarter grades, my friends and I all got C's in gym!

We were amazed. We had never received a C in gym before. After all, we were star athletes (at least in our own minds). When we found out that Ted had received an A in gym, we stormed the coach's office in disgust. Was he crazy? What was up?

The coach was a wise man and, looking back, I can see that he was probably one of my best teachers. As we sat down in his office, he began giving us the lesson of a lifetime. "Yes, Ted did receive an A on his report card," he said. When we questioned that, he said, "You fellas got a C because you did well but only used 50 percent of your ability. Ted, on the other hand, used 100 percent of his ability. Yes, he was slower, but in the end, Ted did more with what he had than you have done. Ted has determination; you boys don't."

It was a valuable lesson for us to learn, and one that has stuck with me throughout all my days since then. I so appreciate that teacher being a mentor to us at that moment. He pointed out our weakness and gave us direction. He couldn't change us; we could only change ourselves.

To help Jennifer learn determination and the ability to "hang in there" when life if tough, we felt we needed to mentor her in two areas. First, that she would determine to follow God and second that she would determine to follow Jesus in spite of the obstacles.

• *Determine to follow God.*

At that time Samuel said to them, "If you are really serious about wanting to return to the Lord, get rid of your foreign gods and your Ashtaroth idols. Determine to obey only the Lord; then he will rescue you from the Philistines."

—1 Samuel 7:3 (TLB)

It was our desire to mentor Jennifer to be determined to follow God. We gave her advice to help her to stand firm and not lose heart or determination. Then, as Jennifer was determined to follow God, so too were her dreams fashioned to follow God's leading. We spent many hours with Jennifer as a child to help her realize her dreams. At first it was to be a singer, then an actress, and then she developed the dream of using her abilities in communications. Each step of the way, we coached and mentored Jennifer to seek God's direction, then, once she received His affirmation, to turn her attention completely on fulfilling God's plan for her life.

Young David faced criticism and ridicule as he went out to face Goliath in battle (1 Sam. 17:1-58). Yet David must have realized that no matter how big the giant may be, God is greater. Likewise, no matter how powerful the giant may be, God is all-powerful. David simply did what God had told him to do, and he didn't melt, even when King Saul laughed at him and his lack of proper armor. Remembering David helps us when we lack determination to hang tough in spite of the circumstances. "It boils down to this: Walking in victory is the difference between what pleases us and what pleases God. Like David, we need to stand fast, to do what is right without tiring of it." [4] That's determination!

• *Determine to follow Jesus, in spite of the obstacles.*

As the time approached for him to be taken up to heaven, Jesus resolutely set out for Jerusalem.

—Luke 9:51 (NIV)

The word "resolutely" carries with it a connotation of standing firm. It means "steadfastly fixing our mind or gaze on something." Jesus knew exactly what He would face. He knew the plan; however, He was steadfast in moving ahead despite the obstacles. Likewise, when God gives us a course of action, we should set our mind "steadfastly" toward those goals. College brought all kinds of new experiences to Jennifer. As we coached her, it was important for us to help her understand that, in spite of obstacles, she needed to pursue God's plan. Paul writes:

Do you not know that in a race all the runners run, but

only one gets the prize? Run in such a way as to get the prize. Everyone who competes in the games goes into strict training. They do it to get a crown that will not last; but we do it to get a crown that will last forever. Therefore I do not run like a man running aimlessly; I do not fight like a man beating the air. No, I beat my body and make it my slave so that after I have preached to others, I myself will not be disqualified for the prize.
—1 Corinthians 9:24-27 (NIV)

Paul is speaking about determination. He knew the prize, and was single-minded in his pursuit of it. No matter what the obstacles, Paul was going to achieve the reward.

He talks about training. For Jennifer, that included being involved in our local church, reading her Bible, and praying regularly. This training helped her keep her resolve, and it gave her the needed input to stay the course.

Paul also tells us not to run aimlessly or beat the air. When we are not determined or we don't coach our children to be determined, they can waste time and effort running without direction. Or, they can simply beat the air and not "connect" with things that really matter. Paul also wrote:

Forgetting those things which are behind and reaching forward to those things which are ahead, I press toward the goal for the prize of the upward call of God in Christ Jesus.
—Philippians 3:13-14 (NIV)

Priorities — Determining What's Important

Helping to set priorities is another important role of the mentor. Often we need to help our kids look at the facts and set their priorities. We must be careful not to simply set them for our children, but we need to help them sort through the facts and then set their own agendas. It's important, as they are bombarded by college, and all that is available, that we give guidance to help them understand what things are the most important.

At times, Jennifer was like a whirling dervish. She had so much to do and so many alternatives. During college she worked, she studied, she attended Bible studies, she attended church, she worked for the church, and she made many friends. She was busy all the time. I can remember many times when we had to sit down together to discuss her priorities. We needed to work with her and help her focus on discovering the right things to do.

Setting priorities and helping our college students focus on them is a threefold process. It helps to use a few simple guidelines like these:

• *Remember that right priorities begin with God.* Proverbs 3:5-6 is Jennifer's life Bible passage. The writer, Solomon, says, "Trust in the Lord with all your heart and lean not on your own understanding; in all your ways acknowledge him, and he will make your paths straight" (NIV). This means turning everything over to God. You can't do this half-heartedly, says Solomon, but you must do it with "all your heart."

Solomon also admonishes us not to lean on our own understanding. The Hebrew verb used for "lean" is *sha'an* and means primarily to support oneself on a staff. Ezekiel 29:6-7 offers a contrast, where we are told about an Egyptian staff *(mash'enet)* that was made out of reeds. Obviously, under any weight it easily broke. The Lord, however, is strong and not like the reed staff. When we set priorities and put God first, we must not lean on our own understanding (made of reeds), but on God.

Lastly, we are told that if we take time to acknowledge (actually, "know") Him, that He will make our paths straight. When we help our kids set priorities, we need to make certain that they acknowledge God and let Him make their paths straight.

At one point, Jennifer had a tough decision to make. She had a great job offer, yet she also had one more semester of college to finish. After much prayer, she decided to take the job, along with a full load of classes. The only way she could do this—have straight paths—was that she fully acknowledged God before she made her decision. Her priorities were straight, and she had the strength and straight paths to do both these things with excellence.

• *Right priorities grow out of consistent dependence on God.* Matthew 6:33 reads, "But seek first his kingdom and his righteousness, and all these things will be given to you as well" (NIV). Before we can help our students as mentors, we must make sure they understand how to set priorities. It starts with having them discover what is really most important to them. "Seeking," in this context, means to discern by thinking, meditating, and reasoning. It really involves thinking things through, praying about them, and reasoning (weighing all the angles).

Once that has been done, our students will come to experience the blessings that come with seeking Him first. This righteousness is the sum total of the requirements of God. Therefore, we help them see His Kingdom and His righteousness. Matthew Henry, a biblical scholar of centuries past, points out:

> *The conclusion of the whole matter is, that it is the will and command of the Lord Jesus, that by daily prayers we may get strength to bear us up under our daily troubles, and to arm us against the temptations that attend them, and then let none of these things move us. Happy are those who take the Lord for their God, and make full proof of it by trusting themselves wholly to his wise disposal. Let thy Spirit convince us of sin in the want of this disposition, and take away the worldliness of our hearts.* [5]

• *Right priorities grow out of obedience to Christ.* Matthew 8:22 says, "Follow me, and let the dead bury their own dead" (NIV). Jesus was asking for some radical obedience in this verse. As we help our kids set priorities, let's convey the importance of obedience to Christ as well.

Mark 2:14 shows Matthew's obedience. In this case, Jesus' call immediately evoked a positive response. Did Matthew know Jesus beforehand? Did other circumstances cause this obedience? Scripture is silent about this. We can only deduce that Matthew followed Christ as a pure act of personal obedience to the Savior. He had seen Jesus, and his priorities grew out of the fact that Jesus had the authority and power to demand obedience. In other words, Christ spoke and Matthew obeyed. Our children need a mentor who helps them set the right priorities for the right reasons. Corrie Ten Boom once said, "When we are obedient, God guides our steps and our stops." As we learn to obey Christ (and help our children to do the same—no matter what age they are), we have full assurance of His hand on every aspect of our, and their, lives.

Accountability—Answering the Difficult Questions

When Jennifer entered college (and perhaps a few months before that), she developed a need to be held accountable. This is much different from normal parental discipline. In fact, I might go as far as to say that accountability is the logical final step as we discipline our children. We move from the role of a disciplinarian parent to the role of a mentor who helps the child understand personal accountability and then remain accountable.

In Luke 10, Jesus sends out His disciples on a "missionary trip." He prays for them, He gives them instructions, He sends them out, and He holds them accountable. He does not set higher expectations than they can achieve, however. He does not compare their results, either to each other or to what He Himself could have done. Nevertheless, He does seek to understand what happened, and He instructs them on what to do next time. That's a wonderful model of holding someone accountable.

For parents to hold their kids accountable involves openness. Both the parents and their kids need to be willing to open up their lives to one another. This requires trust, loyalty, and honesty with each other. Feelings, on both sides, cannot be easily bruised or hurt. Both of us need to allow each other to have the right to examine, question, appraise and give counsel. In other words, the process of developing a young adult's accountability involves vulnerability, teachability, availability, and honesty. It is the final step of the discipline process, and it can bear much fruit for both the parents and the kids.

1. Accountability keeps us from stumbling.

Through presumption comes nothing but strife,
but with those who receive counsel is wisdom. . . .
The teaching of the wise is a fountain of life,
to turn aside from the snares of death. . . .
Poverty and shame will come to him who neglects disci-
pline, but he who regards reproof will be honored. . . .
He who walks with wise men will be wise, but the com-
panion of fools will suffer harm.
—Proverbs 13:10, 14, 18, 20 (NASB)

Solomon was the wisest man in the world, yet as he wrote Proverbs, he insisted on telling us about wisdom and counsel. In our family, Jennifer and Zachary can literally tell us anything. We've moved from the disciplining parent role to that of the mentor who helps them with accountability issues. We encourage, teach, model, and pray with our children in order to help them face the complex issues of adult life. It is our fundamental desire to help them not to stumble before seeking our counsel and the Lord's wisdom for their decisions.

Jennifer bought a car when she was in high school. I was very close to that purchase and worked with her in every step from picking the car, to negotiating price, to taking delivery. When Jennifer was in her last term of college and working full time, she decided to purchase a newer car. In this second purchase, I acted as her mentor. She used me sparingly and negotiated most all of the purchase transaction herself. I did hold her accountable, but my role as a parent with my daughter changed radically during the four years.

2. Accountability helps our kids see the whole picture. Proverbs 27:17 reminds us, "Iron sharpens iron, so one man sharpens another" (NASB). When we don't mentor our kids, they can have a very narrow view of circumstances and life around them. When we come alongside of them as mentors, we can help them expand their horizons and see not only today's viewpoint, but tomorrow's as well.

When we moved to Michigan, we couldn't sell our home in California. It took us eighteen months to finally unload the house. We suffered a severe financial loss of equity and savings. When our wedding anniversary rolled around, we had planned to take a short vacation. However, because of our financial position, we decided to cancel the vacation. Just before I phoned to cancel the hotel reservation, a good friend of mine called. She asked how things were going, and when I told her about our cancelled trip, she said, "Well, what will be more important a hundred years from now?" I didn't completely understand what she was saying, so she went further. "Why don't you and Pam take the kids along with you and 'celebrate' the sold house. Change your plans and just celebrate. In a hundred years the weekend you spend with your kids will mean much more than the memory of a depressed family at a ceremonial occasion."

Therefore, we changed our plans. I used some frequent flyer bonuses, and we went to Niagara Falls. We had a wonderful time and came home to discover that I had earned a small bonus—it more than covered our little weekend trip. One of my mentors had helped me see the world from a macro level, taking my eyes off all the worrisome details. She gave me a glimpse of the whole picture and held me accountable.

3. Accountability keeps our kids from unwise actions. Proverbs 27:6 reads, "Faithful are the wounds of a friend, but deceitful are the kisses of an enemy" (NASB). There are times when we need to love our kids enough to keep them from unwise actions. It can be a bruising time, but we must step in and help them understand that what they are doing is . . . well . . . *wrong*.

Many times parents run away from conflict with their older children. I believe this is because those parents don't understand that conflict is healthy. It's like dynamite—you must handle it carefully, but it can be an effective tool. Using it improperly, of course, can be pretty destructive too!

Conflict was an inevitable part of Jennifer's college years. She was moving toward independence, and we were struggling with letting go. We had many a strong discussion on our family-room couch. However, even with all the tears, we were willing to confront each other, and this allowed us to have a very strong relationship. Did it hurt? Absolutely. Was it worth it? Absolutely. Only by confronting each other could we gain insight into one another's feelings and motivations. Only through confronting could we get past the surface and dig down to the real issues.

The Role of the Empowerer

Empowerment is a business buzzword. It speaks of helping people reach their potential and depends on the leader's ability to transfer "ownership" to employees. Many organizations, from FedEx to Nordstrom, have seen the positive affects of empowering their employees.

The Bible gives us a wonderful picture of empowering. Matthew 28:18-20 (NIV) reads:

> *Then Jesus came to them and said, "All authority in heaven and on earth has been given to me. Therefore go and make disciples of all nations, baptizing them in the name of the Father and of the Son and of the Holy Spirit, and teaching them to obey everything I have commanded you. And surely I am with you always, to the very end of the age."*

The *Leadership Bible* study notes for this verse point out

some helpful principles for using to empower our own families:

• *Be ready to transfer the power!* Jesus let His disciples know He possessed power to transfer to them (v. 18). He had the authority and He chose to delegate the authority to others. We as parents need to make certain that we transfer power to our children as they mature. If we continue to hold the power, they won't feel empowered. They will either demonstrate independence by sneaking around behind our backs, or they will rebel against us. We need to recognize that our "power" changes over time, and we can release it as our children mature.

• *Clearly define the power, and let it be used!* Notice that Jesus commissioned the disciples to use power for specific purposes, which He clearly defined (vv. 19-20). Parents need to allow their children to use the power that has been transferred to them. We also need to clearly define where and when they can use this newfound power. This is especially true in decision-making circumstances. As your kids mature, make sure they know and completely understand when they can be free to make decisions and when they need your help in making decisions. This seems like a small thing, but it is a very freeing concept for growing high schoolers. By the time they enter college, they will be asked to make more decisions than they have ever made before—if you prepare them properly, they will have confidence and know where the boundaries are.

• *Back them up!* Jesus assured them that He would be there to back them up (v. 19). Jennifer knew that, without question, we would back her up. She may even have been wrong, but we never made an issue of it publicly. We also allowed her to "use" us in certain circumstances. She knew we were there to back her up, and if she made a bad decision, we would work together to solve the problem. Kids need to feel they're empowered to make decisions. If we choose to constantly criticize their ability to make decisions, we will be producing adults who have no ability to make good decisions. If we hold them accountable, teach them, advise them, and are standing behind them, they can grow confident in their decision-making skills.

Let me just add one thing. I am not advocating that we bail them out of natural consequences of bad decisions. I believe they need to live by the decisions they have made. We can teach them, however, how to make better decisions next time.

• *Prepare them before delegating!* This is how Jesus operated too (v. 20). As we mentioned in the section on mentoring, it is vitally important to prepare our children through teaching and preparing them. Jesus took three years to prepare these men. He modeled the right behavior and He taught them at every opportunity.

• *Hold them accountable!* Those disciples would be accountable for how they used Jesus' power (Matt. 24:4-51; 25:14-30). Just as Jesus did, we need to empower our children and, once we do that, hold them accountable.[6]

Paul's writings to both Titus and Timothy show us one other trait that we will need to use if we are going to be effective at empowering our college kids. Timothy and Titus were extremely close to Paul. He led them to Christ, and he encouraged and taught them to be ministers of the Gospel. His letters to Timothy and Titus reflect, however, that he didn't empower them the same way. Paul recognized the temperamental differences between Timothy and Titus and he, therefore, adapted his teaching/writing to the needs of each individual.

> *Though written at approximately the same time, Paul's first letter to Timothy is more personal and less official than his letter to Titus. Titus needed clear instructions but Timothy also needed personal encouragement. Thus, Paul encouraged his trusted associate Timothy to stand firm in the faith and not be fearful or intimidated. Paul instructed Titus to "encourage and rebuke with all authority. Don't let anyone despise you." (Titus 2:15, NIV)[7]*

Paul adapted his empowerment to the specific needs of his associates. He didn't take it for granted that they would respond in the same way to the same teaching. Parents must adapt their empowerment to their children's specific temperamental needs (Dr. Kevin Leman would add their birth order, as well). Some kids are Directors and need more freedom than kids with other temperaments. The Thinker will need explanations that are more detailed. Whatever the case, we cannot assume that each of our children is made the same way and will respond the same way to our goal of empowering her to become an effective adult.

The Role of the Navigator

An advertisement contained this quote from Mel Ziegler, founder of clothing retailer Banana Republic:

> *A leader discovers the hidden chasm between where things are and where things would better be, and strings up a makeshift bridge to attempt the crossing. From the other side he guides those who dare to cross his rickety traverse until the engineers can build a sturdier span for all.*[8]

As they grow, our children need guidance on a fairly regular basis. Our role as parents, as they strive to get their lives together and do things on their own, is to find the chasms, coax them across, and build support under them for future crossings (unfortunately, in many issues, it takes multiple crossings). We can help them find their way, we can spot potholes, and we can encourage them though the stormy seas. And for the most part, we are taking the trip right along with them. We can leave them when they are on the right course and they can navigate the rough seas all alone.

In this chapter, we have talked about being a mentor and we have seen what we need to do in order to empower our kids. This final step is to be a navigator. The tasks are clear, but challenging. . . .

• *Navigators plot the course.* They work with their kids to fully understand them and their strengths. They look at their kids' strengths and help them form a plan of where they need to go to be successful and fulfilled. (Please don't misunderstand me, my definition of success here is: *fully using your strengths to the extent that you naturally feel fulfilled because you are working, studying, or playing within your area of strength*). The navigator who plots the course also focuses on what his or her children need to know—how they can be strengthened in life. Finally, the plot includes helping our kids grow.

• *Navigators think ahead.* They help their children see obstacles before the obstacles arise. They think ahead and help their children see problems as opportunities for exercising and strengthening faith. They use common sense, and this common-sense approach takes time to develop. This approach also helps our kids understand that money cannot solve every problem—there are other solutions available. Thinking ahead also gives us an opportunity to coach our kids and help them avoid being overwhelmed by challenges. We knew, for example, that Jennifer would have a hard time on the SAT test's math section. She just doesn't think in a numerical or logical pattern. We tried as best we could to prepare her for the test (we bought some computer software and we managed her expectations), so when she got her results, she wouldn't be absolutely heartbroken. She could look at her non-math scores and be proud of her performance.

• *Navigators make course corrections.* Navigators can help their children learn to be flexible, while maintaining integrity and accountability. They can learn that the plan may change over time and then react to the changes. Jennifer went from ballet to piano to drama. Along the way, we made course corrections to help her develop herself for how she wanted to use her strengths. Had we made her stick with ballet, she would have been frustrated. Making corrections also means helping kids see how far they have come, instead of always focusing on what happened today. Childhood is a significant growth time and it isn't a straight line from babyhood to adulthood. We need to help our children see the continual progress they have made over time. This will instill a good level of confidence in our children and help them reach the next level.

The challenges facing today's college students call for parents who are willing to be navigators—steering their kids away from dangerous seas, focusing them on flexibility, humility, and endurance for the long voyage ahead.

Notes

1 Marian Wright Edelman, "Be Your Child's Mentor," *Parade Magazine*, October 24, 1999, p. 10.

2 *Holman Bible Dictionary* (Nashville: Holman Bible Publishers, 1991). Database © NavPress Software.

3 Charles R. Swindoll, *Living Above the Level of Mediocrity* (Dallas: Word Books, 1987), pp. 93-94.

4 Charles R. Swindoll, *David* (Nashville: Word Publishing, 1997), p. 59.

5 Matthew Henry, *Matthew Henry's Commentary (Concise)* Database © 1996 NavPress Software.

6 This list is found in *The Leadership Bible* (Grand Rapids, MI: Zondervan Publishing House, 1998), p. 1161.

7 Ibid., p. 1425.

8 John Maxwell, *Becoming a Person of Influence* (Nashville: Thomas Nelson Publishers, 1997), p. 144.

ENGAGEMENT–
A TIME TO WELCOME

Chapter 8

I ENJOYED THE FALL SEASON when we lived in Michigan. At some point, usually right around Labor Day, the winds seemed to change. The humidity of summer was whisked away, and when I'd go outside to get the newspaper in the early morning, there was a stillness and crispness in the fall air. Dramatically, but slowly at first, leaves on trees would begin to change colors. Then I'd be startled to see a solitary branch on a huge deciduous suddenly covered with brilliant orange leaves.

Fall was a time of new beginnings. School started, church programs were back on track, and we all heard messages from the pulpit about commitment and vision. And as I drove to work, the changes to the trees would be in full force, ablaze with color. We all knew what was coming, but this special season was a time of beauty and preparation. It was also a time of obligating ourselves to a purpose and positive direction.

Our relationship with Jennifer was entering its own "fall" season. We had come through spring, and then summer, and now we were entering the autumn. We were all being prepared for something, probably the biggest thing we have ever faced together. Jennifer had fallen in love with a young man, and the sound of her voice was romantic, lilting with a smoothness we hadn't heard before. Our daughter was moving on to another phase—marriage—and we were now, together, facing this period known as engagement. Needless to say, it was different for us, and it gave us yet another opportunity to trust God—and also to welcome a new member to our family, Deron Allen Cook.

To get from where we were to this point in our lives was a great journey. We had prepared Jennifer to be an accountable, responsible, thinking human being. She was a college student and working, as well, as a volunteer youth leader at our church. We were excited about this change in her life. We loved the young man who is now our son-in-law, and we realized that, yet again, God was calling us to change—only this time the change included a significant modification of our family.

We successfully passed through this period of our lives by seeking God's strength and relying on His power. We recognized that we were going through a threshold of change to our family, both for us as parents as well as for our daughter. We called upon God through the *power of prayer;* we made good decisions because of the *power of patience;* and Jennifer and Deron launched a successful marriage (making engagement more active than just a proposal ceremony) because of the *power of preparation.*

The Power of Prayer

Jennifer and I have always had a special connection and relationship. Our temperaments are very much alike and we often think alike. In addition, we had spent so much time in play and talking that we had a close father-daughter relationship.

For some reason (and I think our move to Michigan in the middle of her junior year in high school was mostly responsible) Jennifer just didn't date. She had set some high standards for herself, and because of the disruptions in her life, she never found a boy in high school to date. When she entered college, there were some dates, but nothing serious developed.

One day, during my quiet time, I was reading Scripture and I felt as if God were speaking very clearly to me, saying,

"Wayne, you must let her go." I must admit that I didn't understand what God was saying. I had worked very hard to help Jennifer to be self-sufficient and responsible. What was the Lord talking about? I continued to pray and read the Bible, and the Lord revealed His will to me.

After awhile it became very clear: God wanted me to let Jennifer go in the area of dating. I had never stood in her way, but I also realized, with God's help, that I needed to release her, to let her go and be free. It didn't make sense, but I was willing to be obedient and trust God for what He had planned for both of us. Over the next few days, God revealed exactly what He meant by telling me to let go. He was asking me to pray for Jennifer in four areas centered on the subject of dating.

First, I was to pray that Jennifer would meet someone who loved God as much as she did. Jennifer, from early in her childhood, had loved God and committed her life to His care. She was a hard worker at church with the youth and she had sung with me in various worship bands. She was a student of His Word and she prayed and journaled almost every day. Therefore, it was clear. God wanted me to pray that Jennifer would find someone who equaled her love of God and desire to do His will.

Second, I was to pray that she'd meet someone who could love her as much for her weaknesses as for her strengths. In dating we are naturally drawn to a person's strengths. However, over the course of time, those strengths taken to their extreme become weaknesses. The weaknesses inevitably begin to drive us nuts. I think many people give up in marriage because they reach this point and haven't had adequate training in the temperaments to understand their partner's weaknesses. Instead of trying to change them, we need to accept them because of the strengths we so love. God wanted me to pray for a man who would understand and accept Jennifer's weaknesses.

Third, I was to pray that Jennifer would meet someone who would take care of her. Over the course of time, I have seen so many women fall in love and marry men who don't take any responsibilities around the home. They don't work, they don't help, and they take advantage of their wives. My prayer was for Jennifer to meet a team player, someone who would be responsible, hard working, and see marriage as the partnership that it really needs to be for success.

Fourth, I was to pray that she'd meet someone who valued sexual purity as much as she did. We were free with our discussions about sex with both our children. Pam and I had made a decision when we were dating to remain pure, and we hoped and prayed that our children would do so as well. Jennifer had committed herself to abstinence and waiting. She had publicly made a profession of her desire, and my prayer supported her decision.

This exercise in prayer began to radically change me. It opened my heart to Jennifer's needs and it freed me to begin, with faithful anticipation, to see what God was going to do in Jennifer's life. It was exciting, but I didn't share these things with Jennifer until much later.

When Jennifer began dating Deron, it was obviously an answer to my prayers. Deron fulfilled my entire prayer list, and when he came to Pam and me and asked for our blessing to marry Jennifer, what else could we say but "Yes!" God had been so faithful. He had led me to a new discovery, and He had led Jennifer to His chosen person for her. We couldn't be happier.

This was the power of prayer.

God made us and has redeemed us for fellowship with himself, and that is what prayer is. God speaks to us in and through the contents of the Bible, which the Holy Spirit opens up, applies to us, and enables us to understand. We then speak to God about himself, and ourselves, and people in his world, shaping what we say as response to what he has said. This unique form of two-way conversation continues as long as life lasts.[1]

Once again, I had seen the power of prayer, and God had dramatically changed my heart. I was ready to welcome Deron into our family because I had faithfully bathed him and Jennifer in prayer, even before they began dating.

Parents should never underestimate the power of prayer in their children's lives. Any of us can approach the Father and offer up prayers for our children in these ways:

In full assurance of faith (see Heb. 10:19-23, NIV);

With the whole heart (see Ps. 119:58-60, NIV);

With confidence in God (see 1 John 5:14-15, NIV);

With boldness (see Heb. 4:14-16, KJV).

Friends, we can come boldly into the presence of God and get the help we need. No trial is too great, no temptation is too strong, but that Jesus Christ can give us the mercy and grace that we need, when we need it. We don't have to worry that He is too far away. He is right with us, and we don't have to wait; we can go boldly to our loving God. Christianity is the religion of free access to God.

We can go into prayer with God because He is approachable and He completely understands our needs. I could go to God about Jennifer because He knew the answers, He knew how I felt about her, and He could solve the concerns I had for her. He had been there, shed tears for a loved one and let go. And, of course, He wanted the best for His bride—the church.

The Power of Patience

During this time as I was praying, Jennifer was working on patience. As I mentioned earlier, Jennifer hadn't dated significantly in high school. In college, she had several male friends but had never found the right person for marriage. Later, as

Deron was beginning to attract her attention, she needed to learn patience and seek God's direction.

Jennifer and Pam had always communicated about marriage, freely discussing exactly what Jennifer was looking for in a husband. To her credit, Jennifer had a nice list of criteria (just as I did!) for the right man. She needed patience to not compromise this list of qualities that she felt were important to her. After all, she was making a lifelong commitment, and she wanted to make certain that her future husband would be the very one she sought. Jennifer also needed patience, because she was seeking God's direction.

What Is Patience, Anyway?

Jennifer and Deron both worked for our church's youth group, and they shared many moments together in fun and youth activities. Along the way, they became very good friends. But Jennifer wondered: *Should I take the chance of potentially ruining my friendship with Deron by taking it to the next level?*

One day she decided to take the plunge. After a lot of prayer and long conversations with her mother and me, Jennifer decided to ask Deron to be her escort at a friend's wedding. Simple enough, she thought. We will never forget the look on Deron's face when he saw Jennifer all dressed up and ready to go. We knew right then that the relationship had transitioned into something serious. It didn't take Jennifer long, either. Deron's face was beaming—and so was Jennifer's—as they left the house and went to the wedding. They had a great time and, as they say . . . the rest is history.

Yes, your child, too, will need patience during this stage of life. Be ready to mentor him or her by knowing exactly what you're seeking—

• *Patience is waiting for God.* "Rest in the LORD and wait patiently for Him; don't fret because of him who prospers in his way, because of the man who carries out wicked schemes. Cease from anger, and forsake wrath; don't fret, it leads only to evildoing. For evildoers will be cut off, but those who wait for the LORD, they will inherit the land" (Ps. 37:7-9, NASB).

Rest can also be translated "be still." It means for us to just sit quietly and wait patiently or longingly for the Lord. Patience involves endurance, and the psalmist is telling us to just rest easy and wait for His directions.

Most of the time, we just become irritated. "I want patience and I want it NOW!" reads the bumper sticker. We expect the microwaves to speed us along, and we want our computers to blaze faster and faster each year. We have gone from slow phone modems to DSL lines or cable modems with infinitely more speed . . . and still we become irritated. Too slow!

If we become this frustrated with appliances, how do we respond to humans? We're aggravated with them too. However, one of God's favorite methods of teaching us patience is through irritation. Chuck Swindoll writes:

Pearls are products of pain. For some unknown reason, the shell of the oyster gets pierced and an alien sub-stance—a grain of sand slips inside. On the entry of that foreign irritant, all the resources within the tiny, sensitive oyster rush to the spot and begin to release healing fluids that otherwise would have remained dor-mant. By and by the irritant is covered and the wound is healed—by a pearl. No other gem has so fascinating a history. It is the symbol of stress—a healed wound. . . a precious, tiny jewel conceived through irritation, born of adversity, nursed by adjustments.[2]

The psalmist reminds us, "Don't fret, wait on the Lord and you will inherit the land." Jennifer had her list of attributes. She was not going to compromise. Instead, she decided to learn patience and inherit a great husband.

• *Patience means running the race before us.*

Therefore, since we have so great a cloud of witnesses surrounding us, let us also lay aside every encum-brance, and the sin which so easily entangles us, and

let us run with endurance the race that is set before us,
fixing our eyes on Jesus, the author and perfecter of
faith, who for the joy set before Him endured the cross,
despising the shame, and has sat down at the right
hand of the throne of God. For consider Him who has
endured such hostility by sinners against Himself, so
that you may not grow weary and lose heart.

—Hebrews 12:1-3 (NASB)

Running the race before us means we need to develop discipline—a special spiritual discipline that will help us when times get tough. Spiritual discipline does several things for us.

First, spiritual discipline helps us effectively "run the race." Paul, in 1 Corinthians 9:24-27, uses the race illustration to explain that the Christian life takes hard work, self-denial, and grueling preparation. As Christians, we are running toward our heavenly reward. The essential disciplines of prayer, Bible study, and worship equip us to run with force and determination. Jennifer couldn't learn patience in the grandstand. She couldn't just take a couple of laps and have the endurance necessary to be patient. She needed to have the spiritual disciplines in place.

Second, spiritual discipline makes us spiritually "fit." First Timothy 4:7-8 is another message from Paul. This time Paul writes to his beloved Timothy. Paul tells him to spend his time in both physical and spiritual "exercise" in order to stay fit and endure the race. Without good spiritual discipline, it is easy for us to fall into a trap of spiritual laziness. Spiritual laziness can lead to compromise. In order to learn patience we need to endure; in order to remain patient, we need to stay fit.

Third, spiritual discipline strips away the nonessentials. The Hebrews 12:1-3 passage is rich in content. If we focus on it, we can see how it helps us strip away things that are not important and focus on what is. When sprinters run their races, they're focused on the finish line. They get into a rhythm and they totally focus on hitting the tape at the end of the race.

They strip away pain, sweat, their competitors, and the crowd while focusing on hitting the finish line first.

To win the race of patience, we must focus intently on Christ. We must strip away anything that takes our attention off Him. This involves the singlemindedness of the sprinter. Jesus fully understood our pain. He understood our problems. He helped us lay out a plan and does not want us to compromise that plan. He wants our focus, and He wants to teach us patience.

•*Patience brings forth fruits.*

But when the Holy Spirit controls our lives, he will pro-duce this kind of fruit in us: love, joy, peace, patience, kindness, goodness, faithfulness, gentleness, and self-control. Here there is no conflict with the law.
—Galatians 5:22-23 (NLT)

When we allow the Spirit to control us, the resulting fruit is a most pleasing thing to behold in our lives. When we teach our children the value of patience, they can be, under the Holy Spirit's control, not only the recipients of fruit but they can give the fruit to others.

Paul starts with love, because all of the fruits are outgrowths of love. The Greek word here is *agape* and carries with it the pureness of divine love. When persons live in the realm of a loving life, then they also experience joy—that inward calm and personal adequacy that is unaffected by outward circumstances. This type of joy produces an incredibly positive attitude and keeps us going regardless of the circumstance. Love and joy together produce peace. Philippians 4:7 tells us, "the peace of God, which transcends all understanding, will guard your hearts and your minds in Christ Jesus" (NIV).

Patience (courageous endurance without quitting), kind-ness (gentleness), and goodness (*agape*-love in action) are the next three manifestations of living a fruitful life. The Christian who is long-suffering won't waste time trying to even the score or wish trouble on other people who may oppose him. This person will be kind and gentle, even with the most offensive, and will sow goodness (as well as good seed) where others sow evil. Our children should learn that human nature could never do this on its own; only the Holy Spirit produces such results.

The final three qualities are faithfulness (dependability), gentleness (power under control), and self-control (temperance). Each one is a fruit, born from love and available to our children and to us when we learn patience

Jennifer was patient—she waited for the right man to come into her life. We were both prayerful—we prayed for specifics and we prayed that Jennifer would see God's plan for her life. The last power we saw during this welcoming period was the power of preparation.

The Power of Preparation

We were very pleased when Jennifer and Deron joined their church's program for premarital counseling. Pam and I had learned, especially through our study of the temperaments, that you can't learn too much about each other and how you respond to certain pressures and circumstances. Dr. Bill Moore of Trinity Church in Plymouth, Michigan has put together a wonderful program of premarital counseling and our gratitude goes out to him and his staff for what they have done for couples. Dr. Moore provides some insights into his program as he writes:

My approach is that premarital counseling is absolutely necessary today, more so since our young people are approaching marriage with few healthy role models in a world that misunderstands the basis, purpose, and lifelong intent of marriage. I don't think couples approaching marriage can learn a whole lot, since most of them are romantically moving toward the wedding ceremony with little thought to the marriage that will flow from it. However, they can learn a little; and we try to provide some insight and information through a threefold process.

First is the time spent with the pastor. Usually I try to work with them on spiritual things, ensuring that they are Christians by talking with them during the first couple of sessions about their relationship with Jesus Christ. If I think they are unclear or very young in their faith, I will ask that they work through Growing in Christ, a 13-lesson Navigator booklet on Christian growth. I usually ask them to work through three or four lessons each time, and we discuss their answers to the questions in these lessons when I meet with them. During my meetings with each couple, I also administer the Taylor Johnson Temperament Analysis inventory and the Family History Analysis, available from Norman Wright's ministry. Both help a couple to look at each other and their background. Thus they can begin to think a bit more seriously about the ideas and preconceptions (baggage) they will be bringing into the marriage.

The second prong, perhaps the largest dimension of the premarital counseling, is the use of the workbook, written by Norman Wright, Before You Marry. *Usually I will assign the couple to work with an older married couple in our church, a couple with a strong marriage who has been through our training. This mentoring couple will meet with the engaged couple three to five times, usually discussing three or four lessons of the workbook each time. Obviously, the engaged couple must work through these chapters, answering the questions, before the assigned meeting. Usually the mentoring couple will invite the potential newlyweds to their home for dessert. In this way, the engaged couple isn't only working through some extremely important material, they are also forging a relationship with another couple who serves as a role model in marriage and also serves as a caring resource in the years to come.*

The third prong is asking the couple to purchase a number of books dealing with various aspects of married life. There are so many good books on the market today that any combination would be good. The ones I am requiring this year are: Dobson's Love for a Lifetime, *Mike Mason's* The Mystery of Marriage, *Chapman's* Toward a Growing Marriage, *and Penner's* Getting Your Sex Life Off to a Great Start. *I also give the couple a copy of Larry Burkett's workbook on financial planning. With the exception of the last book, of which we were given about 50 copies, I require that the couple purchase each of the other books unless they have them already. My reason is that I want them to have these books in their library for future use as well as current reading. The only exception is if the couple is genuinely strapped for money.*[3]

Preparation Is Something God Appreciates

[1] *Now Moses was tending the flock of Jethro his father-in-law, the priest of Midian, and he led the flock to the far side of the desert and came to Horeb, the mountain of God.*

[2] *There the angel of the LORD appeared to him in flames of fire from within a bush. Moses saw that though the bush was on fire it didn't burn up.*

[3] *So Moses thought, "I will go over and see this strange sight—why the bush does not burn up."*

[4] *When the LORD saw that he had gone over to look, God called to him from within the bush, "Moses! Moses!" And Moses said, "Here I am."*

[5] *"Don't come any closer," God said. "Take off your sandals, for the place where you are standing is holy ground."*

[6] *Then he said, "I am the God of your father, the God of*

Abraham, the God of Isaac and the God of Jacob." At this, Moses hid his face, because he was afraid to look at God.

7 The LORD said, "I have indeed seen the misery of my people in Egypt. I have heard them crying out because of their slave drivers, and I am concerned about their suffering.

8 So I have come down to rescue them from the hand of the Egyptians and to bring them up out of that land into a good and spacious land, a land flowing with milk and honey—the home of the Canaanites, Hittites, Amorites, Perizzites, Hivites and Jebusites.

9 And now the cry of the Israelites has reached me, and I have seen the way the Egyptians are oppressing them.

10 So now, go. I am sending you to Pharaoh to bring my people the Israelites out of Egypt."

—Exodus 3:1-10 (NIV)

In these verses, God told Moses that He had a significant assignment for him. God had heard the voices of the Hebrews and He was going to send Moses to set them free. In other words, Moses was His chosen man of the hour.

For a moment, take a longer glance and look again at verse 1. Moses, the crown price of Egypt at one point in his life, was tending sheep in the desert for his father-in-law. Moses, who assumably would some day have at his command riches, fame, and just about anything he wanted, was tending sheep in the hot desert. J. Vernon McGee writes:

Moses' forty years in Midian have come to an end. All of his schooling in Egypt was not enough to prepare him for his great work of delivering Israel from bondage. God equipped him for this task by forty years of preparation in the desert area of Midian.[4]

Hard work prepared Moses, and through it he gained knowledge in compassion, meekness, contentment, and patience. Moses certainly needed all those qualities and probably many more in order to lead about a million people across the wilderness (see Ex. 12:37). So we can assume that God understands the value of preparation in human lives. After all, John the Baptist prepared the way of Jesus; Paul went into the desert to prepare himself for ministry; God prepared David, who started as a shepherd boy, to be the king of his people. And He prepares us for many missions and challenges in our lives as well.

I have had all kinds of jobs over the years. If you look at them individually, they may seem random or scattered. However, as I look back on my career path, I can see that everything I have done, with all the different assignments and education, has led me to where I am today. I use nearly every skill and lesson from my past job responsibilities. It never ceases to amaze me how I can remember something I did years ago and how it is applicable to what I am doing today. God prepared me for today's job. He took me on His path for what He wanted me to do and accomplish.

I'm simply saying that godly premarital preparation can be a preparation for the future as well. An intimate understanding of what marriage "is" will help couples live out their married years in peace.

Preparation Leads to Peace

¹ So Abijah slept with his fathers, and they buried him in the city of David: and Asa his son reigned in his stead. In his days the land was quiet ten years.
² And Asa did that which was good and right in the eyes of the LORD his God:
³ For he took away the altars of the strange gods, and the high places, and brake down the images, and cut down the groves:
⁴ And commanded Judah to seek the LORD God of their fathers, and to do the law and the commandment.
⁵ Also he took away out of all the cities of Judah the high places and the images: and the kingdom was quiet

before him.

⁶ And he built fenced cities in Judah: for the land had rest, and he had no war in those years; because the LORD had given him rest.

⁷ Therefore he said unto Judah, Let us build these cities, and make about them walls, and towers, gates, and bars, while the land is yet before us; because we have sought the LORD our God, we have sought him, and he hath given us rest on every side. So they built and prospered.

⁸ And Asa had an army of men that bare targets and spears, out of Judah three hundred thousand; and out of Benjamin, that bare shields and drew bows, two hundred and fourscore thousand: all these were mighty men of valour.

—2 Chronicles 14:1-8 (KJV)

Asa was a good king. He followed the Lord's will and he also led his people to prepare against the enemy. He was ready to do battle, and Scripture tells us that he fought with valor.

Any engaged couple faces a tremendous enemy. The enemy is lingering out there waiting to strip away their innocence, their love, and their peace. Good, deeply rooted preparation will help couples learn about each other and face the enemy head on. It will give them the tools necessary to arm themselves and stand firm. In this regard, perhaps nothing hits our children harder than the effects of our society's incredible emphasis on sex.

Since 1994, more than 2.4 million teens between the ages of 15 and 19 have pledged to remain sexually abstinent until marriage, stated a Focus on the Family report on abstinence. "It's a choice to live a moral lifestyle in an immoral world," said Steven Gregg, a youth minister of Forest Park United Methodist Church. He adds, "Kids are having sex in school hallways, on dance floors and in park bathrooms. We are in the midst of sin city. Everything points to sex—topless bars, late nightclubs. Everything on TV, in the movies, and media promotes sex."[5]

We parents need to help our kids focus on living a moral life. We need to help them prepare for the pressure before they face a tough temptation. Jennifer, Pam, and I were always open with our conversations, and we confronted this issue well before Jennifer faced the pressure cookers of romance and engagement. Just like King Asa, we wanted to fortify Jennifer with a wall of knowledge, and we wanted her to know how much we were praying for her whenever she went out. Author Dr. Judith Schwambach, in a personal note to me said:

My advice to engaged couples is to cherish their sexuality by saving it for marriage. If they have been sexually active prior to their engagement, I strongly urge them to immediately put their sex lives on hold and solemnly agree to set aside this invaluable time to devote themselves to literally hundreds of hours of in-depth, utterly transparent, no-holds-barred discussion of every topic under the sun.

Jennifer took an aggressive approach as well. She spent countless hours in Scripture and praying for strength. I realize this doesn't capture the world's view of the romance of engagement, but I believe it is important for us as parents to help our kids when they have taken a positive stand for the Lord, determining to remain pure.

Preparation Involves Prayer

James 1:5 says, "If any of you lacks wisdom, he should ask God, who gives generously to all without finding fault, and it will be given to him" (NIV). We need to help our kids as they prepare by praying *with* them as well as *for* them. We need to encourage them to be prayer warriors for their present as well as their future.

I also felt a new responsibility to pray in earnest for Deron. Before their engagement, I was praying for them as a dating couple, but now I felt called to begin praying specifically for Deron as a husband. I knew firsthand the pressures he would face as a college student and a newly married man, so I lifted him up regularly to God. Welcoming Deron into our family included bathing him in prayer.

Preparation Demands Communication

"Although divorce rates have decreased somewhat from their peak in 1980, estimates indicate that 40 to 50 percent of all first marriages still end in divorce (National Center for Health Statistics, 1988)."[6] Sadly, even people who claim to be born-again don't show a significant difference in their marriages. Christians face an alarming rate of divorce. Dr. Schwambach reminds us, "[Unfortunately], some couples treat the engagement period as though its primary purpose is to plan a wedding. But years of firsthand experience with hundreds of couples have taught me that its primary purpose had better be to determine whether or not there *should* be a wedding."[7]

Many organizations and churches (and the law in many states) are now looking at the value of good premarital counseling and communication. Many recent studies have found that marital satisfaction and success can be predicted on the basis of the quality of the premarital relationship and that marriages can be enhanced and stabilized through strong premarital counseling and communication.

An organization called Life Innovations has conducted several studies on engaged and married couples. They have found that when couples learn about each other and reach compatibility in certain defined areas, that the marriage has a significant chance of survival. "These results [their studies] can provide a starting point for the systematic development of preventative programs that focus on relevant differences between couple types. This study indicates the need to increase the sophistication of divorce—prevention strategies over currently available choices."[8]

Life Innovations has developed a test called PREPARE. It tests couples in the following areas:

Realistic Expectations. This scale assesses the extent to which the individual's expectations about love, commitment, and conflicts in the relationship are realistic.

Personality Issues. This scale examines an individual's satisfaction with his or her partner's habits and behaviors.

Communication. This scale is concerned with an individual's feelings and attitudes toward communication in the relationship. Items focus on the level of comfort felt by the respondent in sharing and receiving emotional and cognitive information from the partner.

Conflict Resolution. This scale assesses the partner's perception of the existence and resolution of conflict in the relationship. Items focus on how openly issues are recognized and resolved as well as the strategies used to end arguments.

Financial Management. This scale focuses on attitudes and concerns about the way in which economic issues are managed within the relationship. Items assess spending patterns and the manner in which financial decisions are made.

Leisure Activities. These scales assess preferences for spending free time. Items reflect social versus personal activities, shared versus individual preferences, and expectations about spending leisure time as a couple.

Sexual Relationship. This scale examines the partner's feelings about the affectional and sexual relationship. Items reflect attitudes about sexual issues, sexual behavior, birth control, and sexual fidelity.

Children and Parenting. This scale assesses attitudes and feelings about having and raising children. Items focus on decisions regarding discipline, goals for the children, and the impact of children on the couple's relationship.

Family and Friends. This scale assesses feelings and concerns about relationships with relatives, in-laws, and friends. Items reflect expectations for and comfort with spending time with family and friends.

Equalitarian Roles. This scale focuses on an individual's feelings and attitudes about various marital and family roles. Items reflect occupational, household, sex, and parental roles. The goal is to discover preferences for more equalitarian roles.

Religious Orientation. This scale examines the meaning of religious beliefs and practices within the relationship. It measures the importance of religion in the relationship.[9]

Whether or not this test is available to your local church or premarital counselor, the topics are invaluable for discussion between your child and his or her fiancé(e). Parents should take a proactive role in helping to foster discussions around these basic areas. Dr. Schwambach adds:

> *Nor would I limit the engagement period to talks with each other. [Couples should] spend as much time as possible with one another's family and friends. Make getting to know your fiancé the number one topic with them. Don't hesitate to ask about your fiancée's strengths and weaknesses. Your goal is "no surprises."*
>
> *If your evaluation period sparks serious misgivings, don't let pride turn your fairy tale walk down the aisle into the kind of stubborn foolishness that forces you to "walk the plank." The temporary embarrassment of wedding postponement doesn't hold a candle to the unending nightmare of marriage to the wrong person. Said Jesus, " . . .you will know the truth, and the truth will set you free (John 8:32)."[10]*

The welcoming time should be a fun time for everyone. As we learn about our new family member, it is a time of prayer, patience, and preparation. Deron is a wonderful man and a fine husband for Jennifer. The night he asked for her hand in marriage is one of the sweetest memories we have. We made certain that our invitation to him was an opening for him to learn about our family and an opportunity for us to learn about him. We took the time to have fun with the engaged couple and to discuss many topics with them. We also made ourselves available to them as they went through the church's premarital counseling program. In other words, we took time to welcome Deron into our family and into our hearts.

Notes

1 *Concise Theology, A Guide to Historic Christian Beliefs* (Foundation for Reformation, 1993).

2 Charles R. Swindoll, *Growing Strong in the Seasons of Life* (Portland, OR: Multnomah Press, 1983), p. 164.

3 Dr. Bill Moore, Senior Pastor, Trinity Presbyterian Church, Plymouth, MI. We owe Dr. Moore a great deal of thanks for his insightful comments and permission to use them in this book. Bill married Jennifer and Deron, and we know that part of their good start in married life is a result of Bill's three-pronged program.

4 J. Vernon McGee, *Exodus*, Volume 1, 1975, p. 37.

5 Denise Carson, "True Love Waits," *The News Herald*, February 6, 1999.

6 Blaine J. Fowers & David H. Olson, "An Empirical Typology Based on PREPARE," *Journal of Family Psychology*, 1992, p. 1.

7 Dr. Judith Schwambach was kind enough to answer questions specifically for this book. The name of her private practice, located in the State of Indiana, USA, is "Compassionate Counsel." She is the co-author of *For Lovers Only*, published by Harvest House Publishers, and writes a weekly Scripps-Howard newspaper column titled, "Your Mental Health."

8 Fowers & Olson, Op. cit., p. 15.

9 Ibid., pp. 3-4.

10 From Dr. Judith Schwambach.

WEDDING—
A TIME TO LET GO

Chapter 9

IN THE MOVIE *FATHER OF THE BRIDE,* Steve Martin sits alone, lamenting the pain of having to let go. Grimacing, as he pronounces his daughter's brand new last name, he says:

> *You have a little girl, an adorable little girl who looks up to you and adores you in a way you could never have imagined.*
>
> *I remember how her little hand used to fit inside mine. How she used to love to sit on my lap and lean her head against my chest. She said I was her hero.*
>
> *Then the day comes when she wants her ears pierced and wants you to drop her off a block before the movie theater. Next thing you know, she's wearing eye shadow and high heels.*
>
> *From that moment on you're in a constant state of panic. You worry about her going out with the wrong kind of guys. Then she gets a little older and you quit worrying about her meeting the wrong guy and you worry about her meeting the right guy. And that's the biggest fear of all . . . because you lose her.*[1]

August 9th, 1997 marked a day that would forever redefine our family. It was a beautiful day for a wedding, and it was a day for another father to lament, as well—me! On that day, our daughter Jennifer married Deron Allen Cook, and the wedding was beautiful. Though I didn't grimace at the thought of my son-in-law (like Steve Martin), the event did mark a time when I had to let go. As I walked Jennifer down the aisle, I smiled bravely for the family and our friends. But inside, my mind was racing with thoughts about letting my precious daughter leave us to set up a home of her own.

The sound of Jennifer's voice on this day was very happy. Her smile was as bright as her future. The little girl who always dreamed of being an actress was center stage in the most important "drama" of her life. She was strong, yet gentle and flowing in her movements. She was bold, yet meek in her speech. She was queen for a day, and we all enjoyed every minute of this beautiful celebration.

As I studied how I was going to learn to let go, God helped me understand that letting go happens *throughout* parenting and that TRUST (Truly Relying Upon Scriptural Truth) was essential to the lifelong process of letting go.

In reality, parents let go almost from the minute of birth. They must learn to let the child sleep in a crib—alone. They must learn to move from the baby stage to toddler (and all of its joyful levels). Parents just get used to the toddler stage and it's time for school and letting go once again to a new environment and a different set of people. School leads to sports, concerts, or church outings, and then it's time to let them drive. Talk about letting go!

Driving leads to dating and graduation. Then "the" event happens, and the family is changed forever. No matter how much we like our children's choice of mate, our family is changed, re-shaped, and different. We would miss Jennifer, but we had to let her go and begin her own life with Deron.

Again, the important thing for all of us parents to remember is that *letting go is a lifelong process*. The events like graduations, weddings, moving out, and all the other major eventualities are just memorial stones. They are times captured in memory with pictures, relatives, and food (for the most part). Trusting God enough to let go, however, is almost a full-time job for the parent. Each stage of child development causes parents to let go of something. Letting go of our children starts early, and we might as well be prepared for it. The sooner, the better.

Rebellion: Refusing to Let Go

Henry Ford was an icon of American industry. His revolutionary ideas about manufacturing and design put him near the top of anyone's list of great American businessmen. The Model T automobile literally changed the face of America and the priorities of its citizens. By 1914, one of Henry's factories built nearly 50 percent of all the cars sold in the USA. When we visited the Ford Museum in Dearborn, Michigan, I was startled to see what this visionary man had accomplished in such a relatively short time.

There was, however, a chink in Henry's armor. He was so proud of his Model T that he never wanted it to be changed or improved. One day, the story goes, a group of his best engineers presented him with a new design prototype. Mr. Ford was so angry with them that he pulled the doors right off the prototype and destroyed it with his bare hands.

It wasn't until 1927 that Ford was willing to change to another model. Grudgingly, in 1927, the Ford Motor Company introduced the Model A. By that time, Ford was well behind his competitors in design and technical advances. In 1931, the Ford Motor Company's market share was down to only 28 percent.

Henry just couldn't let go. He'd created something wonderful but was unable to let it change or improve. He was certain that he had the best ideas for "his" car. Nobody could help him, and he was unwilling to stretch himself to learn about making it better.

At the same time, Mr. Ford undermined his executives, including his son Edsel. As a result, he lost several key people to the competition. You could say that Mr. Ford's attitudes and absolute refusal to see his car change led to rebellion.

Customers rebelled (they bought the competitors' cars), employees rebelled (they got other jobs), and his family rebelled (relations within the Ford family were strained).

In other words, *the consequence of not letting go is rebellion*. Whether you are head of a company and refuse to delegate, or you're a parent who just doesn't want her children to grow and improve, your refusal to "let go" will cause rebellion in your child.

One thing to remember, though—so that guilt won't focus our attention in the wrong direction—is that rebellion and the normal growing-up process aren't the same. Parents have a responsibility to mentor, teach, and motivate their children toward independence. However, at the same time, they shouldn't be riddled with bad thoughts about themselves (in spite of how they have worked with their kids) when the kids show signs of moving ahead to a life driven by their own ability to make decisions—it's part of the process. Our homes need to be a kind of laboratory where we parents develop our kids to become mature, Christ-focused adults. As maturity comes, kids ultimately want to pull away. Naturally, there will be some conflict here! Believe me, this is normal. We want those cute little ones to become self-governing adults someday, right? But that means some friction. And that's okay.

What I'm talking about here, though, is rebellion caused by a parent's refusal to empower and mentor a child. Yes, rebellion is insubordination; however, if parents who are like Ford cause it, then it becomes a choice. Choices can be changed.

Let me give you an example from Scripture. What rebellion is more tragic than Absalom's? Second Samuel 15:1–18:33 gives us the heartbreaking story of what happens when a child rebels and a father doesn't take the time to correct, mentor, and confront.

> *After murdering his own brother, Absalom took refuge in Geshur with his mother's people for three years. Joab, David's general, was eventually able to reconcile David*

with his alienated son, and Absalom returned to Jerusalem. Once back in Jerusalem, Absalom took advantage of his position in the royal family to gain a following, went to Hebron, staged a surprise rebellion, and proclaimed himself king throughout Israel. His strong following posed such a threat that David fled from Jerusalem. David, still a master strategist, gained time through a ruse to organize his forces and put down his son's rebellion.[2]

But what a cost to David's family and to the nation of Israel! In his book on David, Chuck Swindoll writes, "Anger, bitterness, incest, rape, murder, and rebellion among his now-grown children eventually culminated in his son Absalom's leading a conspiracy against him. Is there any pain worse than family troubles?"[3]

David made some bad choices that led to the rebellion of his son. David "had his head in other places" and chose not to spend time with his son. When his son came home for reconciliation, David refused to confront the issues at hand. He made Absalom angry, and this caused even more destruction. David finally refused to take a stand. Here was the man after God's own heart repudiating what he wrote about only a few years earlier. Of course, it's fair to say that Absalom made some bad choices as well. However, I want to make it clear to parents that we set the tone in our homes, and many times our children's bad choices come from our own choices of behavior and habit. Parents need to choose whom they are going to serve.

When Jennifer was in middle school, she began to rebel. She wanted things to happen her way and she was, quite often, unwilling to listen or cooperate. We decided that it was time to help her through this period—and we began to pray for some help! God led us in the right direction and, yes, we went through some additional rough spots. But we all agreed that the choices we made at that time led Jennifer toward being the independent, mature adult she is today. What, specifically, did we do?

• *First, we built on her strengths and needs.* We knew Jennifer's temperament was that of a Director and Socializer. She wanted and needed some control in her life, so we began to give her that control. Her room came first. We stopped nagging about her room and delegated the cleanliness of it to her. It was her space, and we set certain boundaries. But within those boundaries, Jennifer was free to control her own space.

• *Second, we gave Jennifer control of her own finances.* We helped her develop a budget, and we covered her basic expenses. We also said we would cover major needs, like winter jackets. We gave her an allowance (discretionary income) and told her that if she wanted to spend more money on clothes or makeup or whatever, that she would need to earn it. Jennifer loved the concept (being a Director) and went out and found all kinds of jobs. She felt in control, and we were teaching her some basic concepts of responsibility and money management.

• *Third, we confronted Jennifer when we saw questionable behavior.* It wasn't easy (and we'll talk about confrontation later in this chapter); however, it allowed us to discuss and learn about her needs. Often our confrontations prevented major blowups. And this approach gave Jennifer pause: she began to realize that we wouldn't let her just slip away from the course we had all set for her.

I believe the choices we made helped Jennifer make her own right choices. I also believe that the freedom we gave Jennifer within agreed-upon boundaries helped her to feel a sense of personal control. Since she felt some control, she had no reason to rebel.

It's our responsibility to deal firmly with rebellion. It isn't an easy thing to do, but as we saw with David and his refusal to confront Absalom, it's necessary. Yes, it's difficult, heart-rending, and emotional. But in the end, we must stand firm. If we don't stand firm, our family may come under siege from a rebellious, out-of-control child. This may lead to the need for professional help, because nothing should undermine the authority in the home.

Let me quickly add that I'm not recommending abusive behavior or complete authoritarianism. I'm not recommending anything that would damage a normal child's self-esteem. I'm not advocating either extreme. "Letting a child do as he or she pleases (permissiveness) or demanding compliance (authoritarianism)—is lazy parenting."[4] What I am advocating is positive confrontation and standing firm on our basic convictions as parents. When we choose to serve the Lord, when we seek to encourage, and when we try to mentor our kids well, we will face behavioral obstacles and we will need to confront those obstacles. As kids grow, they will get new ideas and challenge us. We need to be ready to confront and stand firm.

The good news is that as we let our kids go, we will see their desire to rebel decrease. Then, more and more independence becomes the order of the day.

Independence: Allowing Control

As I've said, during her teen years we gave Jennifer control over certain things. Her temperament needs to feel in control and we decided to help her become more independent by working with her to create situations where she was in total control. As she grew into a young adult, a natural progression happened: Jennifer became ready to move away from home. I believe our desire to see Jennifer become more independent helped us to let go as well. We had a plan. Sure, on the day she moved into her own apartment we shed some tears. But it was really a culmination of our goal to help her reach her full potential and have an adult's independence.

Jennifer even chose a different church than we did. She enjoyed a certain pastor and group of friends at a different church, and that was yet another step in her growing independence. We had developed within her a mindset to enjoy worship and fellowship with other Christians. Did it bother us that she didn't choose our congregation? Not really. We were extremely happy that she made the decision to be an active member of a great church. She was independent. We had let go. The Gospel of Luke gives us an insight in the childhood of Jesus and the first stirrings of independence from His family:

42 When he was twelve years old, they went up to the Feast, according to the custom.

43 After the Feast was over, while his parents were returning home, the boy Jesus stayed behind in Jerusalem, but they were unaware of it.

44 Thinking he was in their company, they traveled on for a day. Then they began looking for him among their relatives and friends.

45 When they didn't find him, they went back to Jerusalem to look for him.

46 After three days they found him in the temple courts, sitting among the teachers, listening to them and asking them questions.

47 Everyone who heard him was amazed at his understanding and his answers.

48 When his parents saw him, they were astonished. His mother said to him, "Son, why have you treated us like this? Your father and I have been anxiously searching for you."

49 "Why were you searching for me?" he asked. "Didn't you know I had to be in my Father's house?"

50 But they didn't understand what he was saying to them.

51 Then he went down to Nazareth with them and was obedient to them. But his mother treasured all these things in her heart.

52 And Jesus grew in wisdom and stature, and in favor with God and men.

—Luke 2:42-52 (NIV)

In this passage, we learn about Jesus and independence. We all come to certain points as parents. At this time, Mary had to let go of her child and let Him become a man, God's Son, the Messiah. Like most of us, she feared that she hadn't been careful enough with this God-given child; she searched frantically for Him. We can empathize with Mary. How many times do we think we haven't done enough? However, Mary was looking for a boy, not the young man who was in the temple amazing the religious leaders with His questions.

It's hard to let go of people or projects we've nurtured (remember Henry Ford?). It's both sweet and painful to see our children as adults, our students as teachers, our subordinates as managers, our inspirations as institutions. Nevertheless, when the time comes to step back and let go, we must do so in spite of the hurt. Then our protégés can exercise their wings, take flight, and soar to the heights God intended for them.

The important lesson is always to seek what God has intended for our kids. As we work with our children, helping them develop goals and dreams, we must seek out God's wisdom through prayer and study. Once we see patterns (i.e., Jennifer's need for control) we can them help them achieve independence no matter what their age or point of development.

There are several steps we can take to help our children become independent (and help us to see fruit so we feel we can let go). Consider these:

• *Commit to them.* Make a commitment to help them be successful. Get to know their strengths and weaknesses; help them understand their weaknesses and help them develop their strengths. Change your priorities and commitments so you can give your children the time they need to learn. Love for others will always find a way.

• *Believe in them.* Give your kids reason to believe that you trust them and have great confidence in their future. Don't set expectations so high that they could never reach them. Cheer them on, celebrate the victories, and lend them a sympathetic shoulder when they fall short.

• *Be accessible to them.* You can't help them if you're distant or unavailable. So have "an open door" policy. Jennifer and I had some precious moments when I drove her to high school every day. Take advantage of every moment you have to nurture and teach. Even when they get older, remain accessible to your kids; there is still wisdom in your counsel.

• *Offer them opportunities.* We gave Jennifer every opportunity to win. We developed ways in which she could be independent without hurting herself or others. As we saw success, we moved to areas of life that are more difficult. She didn't feel failure was terrible, but we made failure a learning time. Our vision was to help her grow.

• *Lift them to a higher level.* Your ultimate goal should always be to help your kids to a higher level. As they grow, it's easier to let go because you are seeing such progress in their lives. Take time to celebrate and cheer them as they grow into mature adults.

• *Give with no strings attached.* Don't make performance the criteria for success. Helping them become independent doesn't need to be tied to anything but the joy of seeing them develop into great adults.

> *Walt Disney is reported to have said that there are three kinds of people in the world. There are well-poisoners, who discourage others, stomp on their creativity, and tell them what they can't do. There are lawn-mowers, people who have good intentions but are self-absorbed, who mow their own lawns but never help others. And there are life-enhancers. This last category contains people who reach out to enrich the lives of others, who lift them up and inspire them. Each of us needs to do everything in our power to become a life-enhancer, to nurture people so they are motivated to grow and reach their potential.* [5]

As we help our children become independent, we need to focus on helping them move to the next level. We need to be life-enhancers. If we do this, it'll not only help our kids, it will help us let go as well, because we will know we've enabled them to be strong adults.

Freedom: Taking the Next Step

Freedom is the next step after independence. As we work with our kids and begin to let go, they become free. When they reach ages of accountability, our roles as parents change. Whether they are moving out of the house or going off to college, or getting married, letting go involves a transition—they suddenly have freedom.

There are two lessons we need to teach our kids about freedom. These lessons will help them mature and will also help us in the process of letting go.

Find Freedom within God's Boundaries

I am overcome with joy because of your unfailing love, for you have seen my troubles, and you care about the anguish of my soul. You haven't handed me over to my enemy but have set me in a safe place.

—Psalm 31:7-8 (NLT)

God helps us to reach the "safe place." The word used in the Old Testament's original Hebrew actually pictures a broad expanse. God sets us down, not in the camp of our enemies, but in a broad expanse under His complete control. As our kids reach out to freedom, we need to assure them: (1) that God will set them down in a safe place, and (2) God's safe place has boundaries established by Him for our protection.

Some years ago, we attended a Christian camp featuring noted evangelist Luis Palau. We spent the week learning of our freedom within God's Ten Commandments. Dr. Palau taught us that God's commandments were a safe place. Our Heavenly

Father created them for our protection, and He created them to give us boundaries. For example, I am free to love God as much as I want. I am free to love my wife as much as I want. I am free to love my fellow humans as much as I want. There are certain boundaries that come with this freedom—we aren't to love other gods, we aren't to commit adultery, and we aren't to commit murder, be covetous, or tell lies. We are wonderfully free, within boundaries set by God.

As we let our kids go, we have a responsibility along the way to teach them God's boundaries. Our children can be absolutely free and can have absolute assurance of being in a safe place as long as they remember God's boundaries. We ourselves can be "safe" (i.e., not worried about them) if we have the confidence that we choose to teach our children God's boundaries.

Let Christ's Truth Set You Free

Jesus therefore was saying to those Jews who had believed Him, "If you abide in My word, then you are truly disciples of Mine; and you shall know the truth, and the truth shall make you free."

—John 8:31-32 (NASB)

Jesus said that they shall know the truth and it will set them free. He is saying that they will have an intimate knowledge of the truth's power and effectiveness. We had surrounded Jennifer with God's Word. We had family devotions, we had read the Bible at dinner, she had attended church—His life-changing Word surrounded her. As she grew it was so exciting to see her reading the Bible on her own. As she encountered problems, she chose to pick up her Bible and seek God's guidance. She then tried hard to implement the wisdom she'd gleaned. Literally, she knew and acted upon the truth.

The truth had also set her free. As Jesus taught the Jews, He was fighting tradition. It was an accepted belief among many Jews that "no man was free." They were bound by the

Law, and Jesus was trying to help them understand that God's pure grace could free them from their bondage to rules. This is true for our children. The more they understand the message of Christ, the freer they will feel.

During college, Jennifer had an opportunity to spend several weeks in England with a group of students. This was a trip, sponsored by her college, to learn about England's business world. Jennifer was likely the only committed Christian on the trip, and she was exposed to some behaviors that went against her beliefs. The students were not well disciplined, and their evenings were quite . . . *eventful.* Jennifer chose not to participate, and being away from home, she turned to her Bible for comfort. It didn't take long for her to lose her sense of loneliness and be comforted by Jesus. She read the truth and the truth set her free to be herself, in spite of the behavior around her. Jesus set her free.

As we let go of our kids, they will seek freedom. We need to start early in their lives to teach them the boundaries of freedom and the basis on which this freedom is fashioned.

> *Freedom doesn't mean I am able to do whatever I want to do. That's the worst kind of bondage. Freedom means I have been set free to become all that God wants me to be, to achieve all that God wants me to achieve, to enjoy all that God wants me to enjoy.*[6]

Confidence: Depending on God

Letting go should be a process born out of helping our children feel confident. If we can teach them the right kind of confidence, then we can also rest assured that they're moving in the right directions in life with a high self-esteem.

Our kids' self-image is linked to how we act toward them. If we constantly criticize, they will become critical adults. If we tell them they're losers, they'll likely become losers. If they believe they are loved and accepted, they will be much more open to be loving, responsible, respected people.

A child who sees himself as worthwhile and useful [is less likely] to develop destructive patterns. He doesn't turn to drugs and rebellion. He possesses a cooperative spirit, a sense of responsibility, and positive attitudes toward his family. His relationship with his parents is one of mutual trust and respect.[7]

The LORD said to Gideon, "The people who are with you are too many for Me to give Midian into their hands, lest Israel become boastful, saying, 'My own power has delivered me.'"

—Judges 7:2 (NASB)

Gideon lived about 1300 B.C. This was a time when, "the Israelites did evil in the eyes of the Lord, and for seven years he gave them into the hands of the Midianites" (Jud. 6:1, NIV). The oppression of the Midianites was so bad that the Israelites lived in caves. God needed a person to deliver His people. Nobody would have guessed that God's choice would be Gideon. We can learn several lessons from Gideon. Judges 6 is a lesson that teaches us reassurance over our doubts. In chapter 7, the verse above teaches us about the source of our confidence.

God taught Gideon another valuable lesson recorded in chapter 7. Gideon was made general of the army and took a large force of men to fight the oppressive Midianites. God, however, said the praise of victory must be wholly offered to Himself and not to Gideon's personal efforts, and through a process of elimination shrank the army to just three hundred men. The victory could only be the Lord's. Matthew Henry writes:

When the Lord sees that men would overlook him, and through unbelief, would shrink from perilous services, or that through pride they would vaunt themselves against him, he will set them aside, and do his work by other instruments. [8]

God was teaching Israel about dependence on Him. In order to let go effectively, we must practice dependence on God. We must understand it so we can teach it to our children, and we must mentor them in it so when they are on their own, we can trust God enough to let our children go.

Jennifer's confidence was born of her complete dependence on God. This wasn't something she learned overnight. It was a concept (especially for a Director/Socializer temperament) that we had to keep teaching and she had to keep learning. It isn't her natural bent (given a temperament that always wants to take charge) to rely on God, so we needed to help her, model for her, and teach her how important it is to have this kind of dependence. True confidence came from her understanding of the dependence—the more dependent she became, the more confident she grew.

> *Why do the nations rage? Why do the people waste their time with futile plans? The kings of the earth prepare for battle; the rulers plot together against the LORD and against his anointed one. "Let us break their chains," they cry, "and free ourselves from this slavery." But the one who rules in heaven laughs. The Lord scoffs at them.*
>
> —Psalm 2:1-4 (NLT)

God laughs, not at the nations, but at their confused thoughts about power (and confidence). It's the laughter of a father when his three-year-old boasts that he or she can outrun him or beat him in a wrestling match. The father knows the boundaries of power of his little child, and God knows the boundaries of power of the nations. Every nation is limited, but God is transcendent. If you have to choose between confidence in God and confidence in any nation (or in any other person or yourself), choose God! [9]

As parents, we had to put our confidence in the Lord as well. Driving, dating, engagement, and marriage are huge, stressful events. Each one asks parents to let go, give up control, trust the child, and trust God. Just as we had taught Jennifer that her confidence came from God, we had to grow in our understanding of God and have confidence in His plan for our daughter. That way, we could enter into our own new life stage: the empty nest.

Notes

1 From the film *Father of the Bride*, by Touchstone Pictures.

2 Parson's Bible Atlas, Parsons Technology, Inc., 1998. Electronic Edition STEP Files.

3 Charles R. Swindoll, *David, A Man of Passion & Destiny* (Dallas: Word Publishing, Inc., 1997), p. 239.

4. Kevin Leman, *Becoming the Parent God Wants You to Be* (Colorado Springs: NavPress, 1998), p. 169.

5 The list and this quote are from John Maxwell's book *Becoming a Person of Influence* (Nashville: Thomas Nelson Publishers, 1997), pp. 54-55.

6 From Warren Wiersbe, quoted in *Draper's Book of Quotations for the Christian World*, #4122, by Edythe Draper.

7 Don Dinkmeyer and Gary McKay, *Raising a Responsible Child: Practical Steps in Successful Family Relationships* (New York: Simon & Schuster, 1973), p. 48.

8 Matthew Henry, *Matthew Henry's Concise Commentary*, Electronic text and markup, 1995, by Epiphany Software.

9 Life Application Bible Notes, *Life Application Bible* (Wheaton, IL: Tyndale House Publishers, 1991).

THE EMPTY NEST–
A TIME TO REMEMBER

℞

Chapter 10

LABOR DAY, 1997. What a tough day!

As most Michigan families were enjoying the last barbecue of the summer, we were heading to the airport to begin a new life back in our home state of California. What made the day so strange and so complex was the fact that we were leaving our children behind. Jennifer had been married three weeks earlier, and we were leaving Zachary in Michigan to begin his college career.

So many emotions ran through our minds as we sat on the airplane, heading west to our new home. We already missed Jennifer. Even though she had moved out of our house to her own apartment some time ago, we still saw her on Sunday afternoons and occasionally during the week. Now she and Deron were setting up their own home in Madison, Wisconsin, as Deron was about to begin his first year of law school at the University of Wisconsin.

The sound of my daughter's voice was distant.

Continuing to Release

Through our tears and in our conversations, we realized we were standing on a new threshold of our lives. We also realized that we needed to take a firm grip on our Heavenly Father's hand and trust Him for every step of the way.

In the previous chapter, we talked about releasing our kids. For us, this exercise didn't end once we boarded the Northwest Airlines plane to Los Angeles. We found that we had to continue releasing our kids, even as empty-nesters. Releasing became a lifelong process, not simply a one-time event. We had an emotional parting when Jennifer and Deron left for Wisconsin. The next few days were busy for us as we readied our house for sale and, of course, the kids were on their honeymoon. However, as time wore on, we began to miss Jennifer, and it sank in that we wouldn't see her until . . . *Christmas!* This was the longest separation in the history of the Hastings' family. Therefore, we needed to continue releasing Jennifer (and eventually Zachary, as he started his college career).

We had to release repeatedly. We made this discovery because it became so easy to fall back into old roles. One Sunday, Jennifer called and she had caught another cold. She was working hard, and she kept getting sick. Our first response was to fall back into our old roles as her Protective Parents, instead of now being Listening Parents. We jumped to the cry of a sick child, even though our young adult wasn't in real need of our help.

A small road sign in New England says, "Choose your rut carefully, you'll be in it for miles." As we parents move into the era of the empty nest, we need to choose our rut carefully! Like driving on a snow-packed New England highway, finding our way along this developmental road could keep us in a relational rut for a long time. But we did need to choose a new rut, one that would help us continually leave things behind. One that would allow us to experience the new freedom of our new role. This rut would need to have at least two "wheel tracks" in it: grieving and celebrating.

Grieve—It's Okay!

Because she loves traditions, Pam created many special moments for our family over the years. It seems that every holiday, every birthday, and every other milestone was thoroughly celebrated and enjoyed. Our family had a huge scrapbook full of wonderful, joy-filled memories.

Now we faced a future where many celebrations wouldn't include our kids. We would now spend some holidays, some birthdays, and some important events apart from each other. Christmas of 1999 was a great example. Because of Deron's law school final exam schedule and Jennifer's employer's fear of impending Y2K problems in his business, our newlyweds couldn't visit us for any part of that Christmas season. For the first time in many years, we would celebrate Christmas without our daughter.

Through all the tears that came with this and other disappointments, both of us came to the realization that it was okay to grieve the "loss" of our kids—the way things used to be with them. Zachary and I are very close, as well, and music has always been one of our strongest bonds. We played in several praise bands together, and we have shared the stage in performing special music in church. In the beginning of our separation, it was almost impossible for me to hear the songs we had performed together without crying and longing for him to be with me.

As a child, Jennifer enjoyed *Little House on the Prairie*. In a few short years, we read the books to her, then she read the books, and we all enjoyed the television series. Now I found myself hating to see the re runs. I remember being on a business trip and turning on the television late one night just to unwind from a long day. I flipped through the channels, and there were Laura and Pa Ingalls. I immediately broke down, awash in a flood of memories about "Pa" and Jennifer.

Pam had similar experiences. She and Jennifer were best friends, and Pam so missed Jennifer for girls-only outings and shopping (two of their favorite things to do). Pam and Jennifer also liked to cook together, and on some days the absence of laughter and fun in the kitchen (as they whipped up something special) pierced Pam's heart with a deep sadness.

As we talked, it became obvious that we were looking at

this period of our lives in the wrong way. I am a Director temperament at heart, and it isn't my first reaction to cry. Pam, the Thinker/Relater, has an emotional bent, but both of us were feeling that we were overdoing it. On the other hand, as we talked, we realized that we'd be wrong to hide our feelings. It was reasonable to expect that we'd miss our kids and we knew we needed to grieve. We found that intentionally grieving could act as a medicine and indulging in memories were a kind of tonic. C.S. Lewis once wrote, "The great thing with unhappy times is to take them bit by bit, hour by hour, like an illness. It is seldom the present, the exact present, that is unbearable."[1]

Consider how it was with the biblical David and his grief for a beloved friend and his father . . .

> [5] *"How do you know that Saul and Jonathan are dead?" David demanded.*
> [6] *The young man answered, "I happened to be on Mount Gilboa. I saw Saul there leaning on his spear with the enemy chariots closing in on him.*
> [7] *When he turned and saw me, he cried out for me to come to him. "How can I help?" I asked him.*
> [8] *And he said to me, "Who are you?" I replied, "I am an Amalekite."*
> [9] *Then he begged me, "Come over here and put me out of my misery, for I am in terrible pain and want to die."*
> [10] *"So I killed him," the Amalekite told David, "for I knew he couldn't live. Then I took his crown and one of his bracelets so I could bring them to you, my lord."*
> [11] *David and his men tore their clothes in sorrow when they heard the news.*
> [12] *They mourned and wept and fasted all day for Saul and his son Jonathan, and for the Lord's army and the nation of Israel, because so many had died that day.*
>
> —2 Samuel 1:5-12 (NLT)

This wouldn't be the last time that David tore his clothes in grief, but it shows how he dealt with hearing of his king's and his best friend's deaths. David and his men freely expressed their sorrow; they tore their clothes as they demonstrated an outside manifestation of their grief. In so doing, they were able to express their deep emotion freely and in such a way that it helped them to become much stronger.

Sometimes the healing process isn't as immediate, though. In her book *Roses in December,* my friend Marilyn Heavilin tells this story:

> *More than two and a half years after [our son] Nate's death, I started to play a cassette tape of myself which I had recorded when I was speaking at a luncheon a few months earlier. I inadvertently placed the tape into the recorder on the wrong side. I listened to the woman speaking and thought, "Who is that? This isn't my voice."*
>
> *As I listened, I heard a piano and a male voice. I quickly realized I had discovered a tape of one of Nathan's voice lessons! I prayed, "Oh God, please let me hear him clearly; don't tease me with this." As he began to sing, the teacher suggested he move closer to her, which was also closer to the tape recorder. I could hear him perfectly, God answered my prayer!*
>
> *I sat on our living room floor sobbing as I heard Nate sing one song and discuss it with his teacher. She asked, "Nate, do you have any more songs?"*
>
> *He answered, "I've got one more. It isn't my favorite, but it's my mom's favorite and I want to learn it for her!"*
>
> *I felt I had moved back in time, back to when things were normal, back when I couldn't comprehend how much emotional pain one body could stand. I hungrily devoured each precious note as Nate sang the beautiful, Jewish-sounding melody, "Pierce My Ear, O Lord."[2]*

Marilyn and her husband Glen understand the importance

of the grieving process and its role in healing. God gave them a gift in this tape, and it, along with friends and the impact Nate's death had on the local community, helped them through the process. They never will forget their loss, of course. The pain remains. However, their expression of grief, like David's, helped them through the process of getting on with their lives. They were not ashamed to grieve, nor did they consider grief a sign of weakness. The expression of grief can help us with our intense sorrow. And sometimes, like Marilyn, we receive a little rose in December.

During our transition to the empty nest, Pam and I needed to pray together like at no other time in our lives. We would express our sorrow and then move to prayer. God couldn't change our circumstances; however, he could change us, and that is exactly what we needed Him to do. Nehemiah 1:2-4 (NIV) says:

> *Hanani, one of my brothers, came from Judah with some other men, and I questioned them about the Jewish remnant that survived the exile, and also about Jerusalem. They said to me, "Those who survived the exile and are back in the province are in great trouble and disgrace. The wall of Jerusalem is broken down, and its gates have been burned with fire." When I heard these things, I sat down and wept. For some days I mourned and fasted and prayed before the God of heaven.*

The situation in his homeland tore deeply into Nehemiah. Instead of just waiting for something to happen, Nehemiah decided to act—

• *Nehemiah prayed.* He poured out his heart to God and sought God's help in finding a solution.

• *Nehemiah considered.* He put all he knew into finding the right solution and moving forward.

• *Nehemiah acted.* He approached the king and sought to go back home to build the wall.

When we enter the empty nest period, we need to grieve

our loss. We will miss our kids, and we will miss the blessings they bring to us. The house will be quiet (I know you may be saying "Amen" right about now but, believe me, it gets a little *too* quiet) and you realize that a time in your life is passing away. You need to grieve. You need to express your feelings to God and see how He wants you to grow. You need to move to prayer and action with your spouse.

You also need to celebrate the past.

Celebrate — That's Okay Too!

¹ When all the people were safely across the river, the LORD said to Joshua,
² "Now choose twelve men, one from each tribe.
³ Tell the men to take twelve stones from where the priests are standing in the middle of the Jordan and pile them up at the place where you camp tonight."
⁴ So Joshua called together the twelve men
⁵ and told them, "Go into the middle of the Jordan, in front of the Ark of the LORD your God. Each of you must pick up one stone and carry it out on your shoulder— twelve stones in all, one for each of the twelve tribes.
⁶ We will use these stones to build a memorial. In the future, your children will ask, 'What do these stones mean to you?'
⁷ Then you can tell them, 'They remind us that the Jordan River stopped flowing when the Ark of the Lord's covenant went across.' These stones will stand as a permanent memorial among the people of Israel."

—Joshua 4:1-7 (NLT)

These special stones that Joshua commanded the men to bring into camp would be a vivid reminder of what God had done for the people of Israel. God had delivered them out of slavery; He had provided manna for them (in fact, He met all their needs for many years of roaming in the desert). God gave them the Ten Commandments. He took them across two rivers with dry feet and placed them safely on the other side. The Israelites had much to remember.

We have much to remember as well. I've said before that Pam loves tradition. She has created for our family some simple, yet wonderful traditions that we will never forget. One silly tradition we have is Christmas pajamas. When the kids were young, we started giving them pajamas on Christmas Eve. Each year, they knew at least one present they would receive: new PJs. The tradition expanded as we went to church on Christmas Eve and came home to open a few presents. They would open their pajamas and we would enjoy our Christmas Eve together with a helping of peppermint ice cream and homemade chocolate fudge sauce.

As the kids grew older, we thought the tradition would slowly go away. Boy were we wrong! Christmas of 1999 found us celebrating without Jennifer or Deron—they had to stay home in Wisconsin. However, they reminded us that they were expecting the annual PJ present (they also wanted the dessert, but it's pretty hard to mail ice cream).

Parents, don't ever underestimate the power of memorial stones, of celebrating your memories of the past. Matthew Henry, writing about the Exodus verses says, "The works of the Lord are so worthy of remembrance, [sic] and the heart of man is so prone to forget them, that various methods are needful to refresh our memories, for the glory of God, our advantage, and that of our children. God gave orders for preparing this memorial."[3] We might paraphrase his comments to say that the works of the family are so worthy of remembrance. We need to take special care of our memories and celebrate all of our important events.

As we go through the empty nest period, it is wonderful to celebrate where we have been and how God has blessed us. Part of our celebration process has been to thank God for our children and the absolute blessing they brought into our lives. We wouldn't be the people we are today if it hadn't been for our kids and we shared some incredible moments with them as they grew up. Therefore, we spend time celebrating the past.

Building on the Past—With Contentment

Not that I have already obtained it, or have already become perfect, but I press on in order that I may lay hold of that for which also I was laid hold of by Christ Jesus. Brethren, I don't regard myself as having laid hold of it yet; but one thing I do: forgetting what lies behind and reaching forward to what lies ahead, I press on toward the goal for the prize of the upward call of God in Christ Jesus.
— Philippians 3:12-14 (NASB)

God doesn't want to take away the past. It's a vital part of all of us. He does, however, want us to look to the future and all the new blessings He has in store for us. Paul talks about pressing toward the goal. We empty nesters need to build on our past and then move to a stage of pressing ahead. The biblical Greek word for "press" is *dioko,* and it means "speeding on earnestly to win the race." We need to speed on, building on the wonderful memories of the past, while seeking God's new direction in our lives. God gives us the ability to build on our past as we celebrate it.

And all of this begins to bring us great contentment. An old proverb says, "Contentment isn't the fulfillment of what you want, but the realization of how much you already have." As we continue to release and learn to celebrate this new part of our lives, we need to move into a sense of contentment. Pam and I are experiencing a fresh new married life as we enter the empty nest. We're learning new things to enjoy together and we feel the freedom to do many things that we couldn't do when our children were at home.

Easton's Bible Dictionary defines contentment as, "A state of mind in which one's desires are confined to his lot whatever it may be."[4] This reminds me of two great Scripture passages: "But godliness with contentment is great gain. For we brought nothing into the world, and we can take nothing out of it" (1 Tim. 6:6-7, NIV) and "God is able to make all grace abound to you, so that in all things at all times, having all that you need, you will abound in every good work (2 Cor. 9:8, NIV). William Barclay writes:

> *Contentment comes from an inward attitude to life. In the third part of* Henry the Sixth, *Shakespeare draws a picture of the king wandering in the country places unknown. He meets two gamekeepers and tells them that he is a king. One of them asks him: "But, if thou be a king, where is thy crown?" And the king gives a great answer: "My crown is in my heart, not on my head; Not deck'd with diamonds and Indian stones, Nor to be seen; my crown is call'd content—A crown it is that seldom kings enjoy." Content comes when we escape the servitude to things, when we find our wealth in the love and the fellowship of men, and when we realize that our most precious possession is our friendship with God, made possible through Jesus Christ.[5]*

Contentment flows from our heart attitude, not our circumstances or the things we have around us. As we learn to release our kids and celebrate the past—the memories we have created—we can move toward contentment and focus upon what new adventures God had planned for us. The psalmist writes:

> *O Lord, my heart isn't proud, nor my eyes haughty; nor do I involve myself in great matters, nr in things too difficult for me. Surely I have composed and quieted my soul; like a weaned child rests against his mother, my soul is like a weaned child within me. O Israel, hope in the LORD from this time forth and forever.*
>
> —Psalm 131:1-3 (NASB)

He rests in the Lord and encourages us not to spend any time in things that are great or difficult. This isn't an indictment against being involved in challenges or hard projects; rather the psalmist is telling us not to consume our days in worry. We can trust God. We can relax.

Pam and I have noticed something significant in this regard. When our kids come home for a visit, it appears that they are looking for something. I think that they, too, miss the past memories—the way things used to be—and they're seeking to return to a calmer time. When Jennifer comes home, she totally relaxes. Gone is the pressure of working full-time and the pressure of balancing her busy life. She just relaxes and "flops" into an easy chair. We can almost hear an audible sigh of complete relief.

At this time, we try our best to create a safe harbor. I have always told Pam that she created a "safe harbor" for me, and now I see the importance of doing that same thing for our children when they come home. We create a safe, fun place of refreshment and relaxation for them. We try to allow them to rest and regain the strength they have lost through working, studying, and being young adults in a fast-paced society. We want our home to be a refuge.

The Book of Proverbs says, "He who fears the LORD has a secure fortress, and for his children it will be a refuge" (14:26, NIV). God asks us parents to "fear" Him. The word means, "be in awe of." We should reserve a special place for God and respect all He has done for us. Once we do that, we can provide our kids with a refuge.

Refuge, in this proverb, is the Hebrew word *mehseh*. It pictures "taking shelter from a rainstorm" (see Isa. 4:6; 25:4; Job 24:8) or from danger in the high hills (see Ps. 104:18).[6] The idea comes from the plight of soldiers who needed to flee an enemy. They would run into the hills and seek rocks or caves in which to hide. They felt helpless and needed a "safe harbor" from the danger. As we move from having children at home to being empty nesters, we can be content to help our children seek their own *mehseh*. No matter what they are dealing with in their jobs, in college, or in their own families, we can be their safe harbor and give them shelter and a time of rest.

One other thing: as we help our kids find contentment and peace, we will come to a place of real contentment *with ourselves* too. Pam and I now feel free to do things that we couldn't do when we had our kids at home (writing this book, for example). Our relationship has grown to a new level of love and joy as we can take time to focus on each other and actually dote on each other. We have special date nights and, many times, Pam is free to travel with me when I go on a business or speaking trip.

We find our level of communication is much higher than ever before. We have time for walks, talks, and praying together. We take time to be silly and we are free to enjoy each other's company in ways we hadn't been able to do since before our kids were born. In the past, my time after the workday was devoted to playing with our kids, or working on projects with them. Now my time is with Pam, and we're enjoying this newfound time as a gift.

Sure, at times we struggle with this new role. However, we are learning to let God take care of our new circumstances. When Deron graduates from law school, he and Jennifer will be relocating in Cleveland, Ohio. Now, there isn't a thing wrong with Cleveland, and we are very proud of his accomplishment, but Cleveland is two thousand miles away from California. This brings into our lives yet another new circumstance of the empty nest.

Finding a New Future

[1] The LORD had said to Abram, "Leave your country, your people and your father's household and go to the land I will show you.
[2] I will make you into a great nation and I will bless you; I will make your name great, and you will be a blessing.

3 I will bless those who bless you, and whoever curses you I will curse; and all peoples on earth will be blessed through you."

4 So Abram left, as the LORD had told him; and Lot went with him. Abram was seventy-five years old when he set out from Haran.

5 He took his wife Sarai, his nephew Lot, all the possessions they had accumulated and the people they had acquired in Haran, and they set out for the land of Canaan, and they arrived there.

6 Abram traveled through the land as far as the site of the great tree of Moreh at Shechem. At that time the Canaanites were in the land.

7 The LORD appeared to Abram and said, "To your offspring I will give this land." So he built an altar there to the LORD, who had appeared to him.

—Genesis 12:1-7 (NIV)

This story of Abraham (earlier in his life he was called Abram) is a stirring example of someone called to find a new future. God told Abraham to leave his secure, reasonably known life behind and to strike out for a brand new place. Abraham didn't have the opportunity to learn about this adventure, to call his local travel agent and check out all the details. He just went because God called him to go. As we enter the empty nest, we can learn several lessons from Abraham.

Even though he knew nothing of what was before him, Abraham was able to trust God much further than he could see Him. His obedience was speedy and immediate. Hebrews 11:8 (NIV) reminds us, "By faith Abraham, when called to go to a place he would later receive as his inheritance, obeyed and went, even though he did not know where he was going." This verse tells us that Abraham submitted to God and obeyed. The result was: he went.

Too often the trap of *not* obeying and trying to stay right where we are trips us up. We get so involved in our own worlds that we fail to see the blessed new "world" God is offering us. The empty nest presents incredible opportunities for us to move into vast, uncharted areas of our lives. What an adventure! We can serve our local church, we can rekindle our marriage, we can do those projects we always wanted to do, or we can just sit and relax with a cup of coffee. Whatever our decision, we need to be like Abraham: let's go!

Because of Abraham's obedience, God blessed him. His obedience led him to new assurances and new promises from God. Abraham became the father of a nation and was given the gift of the land. God blessed his obedience and trust with something Abraham couldn't have even imagined if he had stayed where he was. This portion of Scripture points out six blessings that Abraham received:

I will make you a nation (12:2);
I will bless you (12:2);
I will make your name great (12:2);
You will be a blessing (12:2);
I will bless those who bless you, curse those who curse you (12:3);
To your offspring, I will give this land (12:7).

Abraham's obedience led to blessings that not only affected him personally but had impact for generations to come. There is no hint of conditions here. Abraham had demonstrated his faith by obeying God's command to leave his homeland, and he received blessing.

Most of us aren't asked to pull up stakes and go to a strange country, but the challenges of facing an empty nest are just as real. Sometimes there are serious problems in the home, on the job, or in the church; and we wonder why God has permitted these things to happen. However, when we obey and submit to God, we will see a blessing in our lives. While we are going through the circumstance or change, we may struggle within a fog of misunderstanding, but God is always faithful. He is always there with us. If we allow it, the empty nest can be a blessed new adventure filled with thrilling opportunities. That is my prayer for you.

> [11] *"For I know the plans I have for you," declares the LORD, "plans to prosper you and not to harm you, plans to give you hope and a future.*
> [12] *"Then you will call upon me and come and pray to me, and I will listen to you.*
> [13] *"You will seek me and find me when you seek me with all your heart."*
> —Jeremiah 29:11-13 (NIV)

Notes

1 Walter Hooper, *C.S. Lewis: A Companion & Guide* (San Francisco: HarperSanFrancisco, 1996), p. 297.

2 Marilyn Willett Heavilin, *Roses in December* (Nashville: Thomas Nelson Publishers, 1993), pp. 41-42. Marilyn's son Nathan was killed by a drunk driver, February 10, 1983.

3 Matthew Henry, *Matthew Henry's Concise Commentary*. Database © 1996 NavPress Software.

4 *Easton's Bible Dictionary*. Electronic text and markup copyright 1995 by Epiphany Software.

5 William Barclay, *Daily Study Bible—New Testament* (Louisville: Westminster John Knox Press, 1975).

6 *Theological Workbook of the Old Testament* (Chicago: Moody Press, 1980). Electronic text and markup © by Epiphany Software.

THE SOUND OF MY FATHER'S VOICE
A Daughter's Last Word

Epilogue

From the moment I met my Dad, I loved him. We have always had a special bond—father and daughter. I don't remember the first time I heard my dad's voice—I just always remember it being there. Whether his tone communicated love, support, guidance, even disappointment, the sound of my father's voice touched my heart like nothing else. As a little girl, people could see that I resembled my dad; so much so that I was called "Little Wayne." "Thank you," my dad would reply, his voice filled with pride and joy. How lucky I felt to know that Dad was proud to have a daughter who looked like him.

We often spent the evenings together. I would wait anxiously to hear Dad's voice after he came home from work, because that meant he would be my playmate until bedtime; we had a whole evening to spend together. Dad always drank my tea when we played "tea party" and was my favorite customer at "Jenny's Store." As my voice came alive with all sorts of different characters conjured from my imagination, his laughter would fill the room, causing all sorts of silly reactions from me.

Dad and I loved to sing our favorite songs together too. His guitar spoke of the happiness of the moment, of being together and sharing in music. Nothing was more important in my childhood than knowing that with one sound from Dad, all the scary dreams and nightmares lingering in the night would vanish. Whenever I called his name, he would be there with a hug of comfort to give and a voice that comforted me and helped me back to sleep. His actions reflected his words. By far, the sweetest tones of his voice came when he would say "I love you," and without a thought, I would reply, "I love you too, Dad." I learned to hear my dad's voice, and in listening we became friends.

There were times when Dad's voice sounded like the coach of a sports team, combining both encouragement and discipline. I grew up with parents who knew I could do anything to which I set my mind. "You can do it," and "Don't be afraid to try," were common cheers heard whenever I struggled with some new task or situation. If I was thinking "I can't," what inspired me to try again was the sound in their voices that said, "We won't let you fail. We are here to help you."

I accomplished many new ventures in my life because my cheering section never gave up! Being a redhead, trouble seemed to find me, so I knew the tone in my parents' voices that meant I was in trouble—especially when I heard my *full* name ring out for some act of disobedience. However, I wasn't frightened by the sound of my name at those times. I just felt convicted. We had a policy in our house that no one was to strike or speak out of anger. Voices might have been raised, and for good reason. Yet growing up, I knew that after appropriate punishment, I would receive a hug, and the tense tones of my parents' voices would return to the sound of the coach saying "You can do better, and we will help you to see that."

Dad was a magical storyteller, and nightly story time was a favorite ritual of mine. Reading and sharing stories together turned my thoughts in imaginative spins. There were many books that I wanted read over and over, just so I could hear Dad's different inflections. His voice would take me on magical journeys to faraway places, right from our living room.

Family Bible study was also a vital part of our family life together. I eagerly looked forward to hearing Dad read stories from the Old Testament and promises from the New Testament. This was a time of peace and instruction at the close of our day. Dad was able to make the Bible characters come alive, and it was fun to discuss specific persons and think about how we could apply their lessons to our lives as a family.

Prayer time followed. I fondly remember hearing the prayers of my parents. Whether it be on some issue in particular that I asked them to remember, or just their words of encouragement through prayer, I always felt as if their voices were reaching up to heaven and touching the very ears of our Lord. When Mom or Dad said, "We are praying for you," I knew that was a promise they would keep.

Through Dad's example of faith, I was introduced to the Lord. The sound of his voice talking to God, memorizing Scripture, and asking God for help in all situations showed me that I could talk to Him just as my dad did. The sound of my earthly father's voice was well known to me. It is where I found comfort, laughter, and security.

It was also through his voice that I established a relationship with my Heavenly Father and began to hear His voice. I knew that my parents loved me, that no matter what I did, they would always be there for me. I learned to trust them, realizing that they held my best interest in their hearts. When I met the Lord at the tender age of five, I had no problem knowing and feeling His love for me because of the wonderful bond He had given me with my parents. Our relationship was a precious reflection of the relationship I could have with my Heavenly Father, a fact very clear to me even at such a young age.

During my high school and college years, the bond between Dad and me changed. The days of tea parties and story times were precious memories, yet I discovered a new way to communicate and hear Dad's voice. When I brought troubling stories to him of temptations I faced or difficult situations I was experiencing, his voice of calmness reminded me that all would work out in the end. I even discovered that he had faced many similar experiences, and I learned that he was a source of advice and a safe place just to express my feelings.

My Heavenly Father served the same purpose on even a greater level. My parents modeled the importance of having a prayer journal, and during those struggling times of growing up as a Christian young woman, I found real strength in talking to my Lord as if I were talking to my dad. As I began my own prayer journal, my heart heard the calming voice of God, guiding, directing, reassuring, and disciplining—always loving. My dad took seriously his role of parenting me to be the woman of God he knew I could be.

Nevertheless, he did have to leave some of that responsibility to the Lord and me! I had to make the choice to either follow the voice of the crowd, the voice of my parents, or the voice of God. Several times I heard all three voices at once, and I felt as if I had come upon a crossroad where one wrong turn would lead me down the wrong path. In those times of struggle, it was comforting to rely upon my relationship with my Lord and my parents, to choose their voice over the crowd, to trust that they would see me through any difficult time.

Just a few years ago, a new voice entered my life, the voice of my husband, Deron. About a year before Deron entered my life, my dad calmly informed me that he was praying that I would meet someone to share my life with, to share the same type of relationship he has shared with my mom for more than thirty years. My reaction to his statement was strange and a bit puzzling. Dad's voice was the only male voice I much trusted, especially after a string of girlhood crushes that never lasted. I realized then that even though my heart's desire was to marry, I did not want to lose my ability to hear my dad's voice nor the special connection that he and I share as father and daughter.

My Heavenly Father heard the prayers of Dad, though! Two short years after that conversation, Deron and I were married. The "Mrs." now attached to my first name has not changed the fact that I still need to listen to the voices of my dad and my Heavenly Father. The wonderful thing about marriage is that it shows just how little we really know about spending our lives with another person.

Dad's voice has become one of mentor and friend. It is easy for me to relate a story or two about my life as a wife because I am still his daughter. Dad isn't raising me anymore to become an adult, yet I rely on his advice as I would a mentor, finding comfort and strength in his perspective. Since we live 2,000 miles away from Mom and Dad, it is their voices that greet me every Sunday night on the telephone, just to catch up. Not being physically close to them has been an adjustment for me. We have learned to pick up the phone and call for even the most boring of bits of news, just to hear each other's laugh.

My parents are still always there to listen. My prayer life with God is much the same—"Just me, God, needing to hear Your voice"—and I find even the most urgent of life's concerns is solved when I bring them before my Father. I can rest assured that He is always listening.

The gifts my dad has given me in my lifetime are endless in number. He has given me his time, his prayers, his support, his encouragement, his discipline, and his strength. The importance of my dad's voice in my life cannot be measured, because the involvement of my parents has helped shape me into the woman I am today. In a hurried world that focuses only on the moment, it is vital to remember that we each have an eternal soul and that spending time together is most precious. My dad's voice brought me to the point of being able to hand my eternal soul over to God, which in turn began a lifetime partnership between God and me.

One day I, too, will be able to hand my children's souls to the Lord, and what was started with my parents will continue through each generation. What a legacy to share! I encourage the parents reading this book to realize the special sound of their voices to their children. Those young ones so want to hear from you, to help them grow and develop.

Many voices surround each of us, but for me, it is my dad's voice that rings so sweetly. And it is my Heavenly Father's voice that rings eternal.

PARENTHOOD:
NOT A JOB FOR THE FAINTHEARTED.

IGNITE THE FIRE

10 ACTIONS TO MOTIVATE YOUR KIDS TO PURSUE JESUS.

ISBN: 1-56476-747-7

"What can I do to help my children turn out right?"

Find out by reading *Ignite the Fire*, written by popular youth ministry speaker Barry St. Clair and his late wife, Carol.

Other Faith Parenting Titles

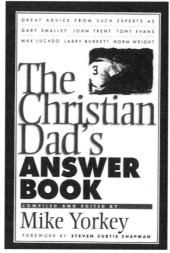

The Christian Dad's
Answer Book
0-78143-364-9

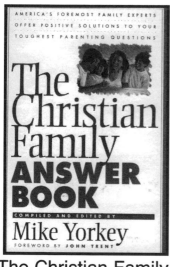

The Christian Family
Answer Book
0-78143-362-2

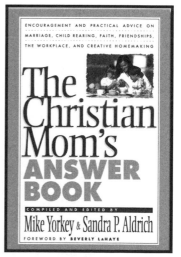

The Christian Mom's
Answer Book
0-78143-363-0